Rainer Maria Rilke

Also by
DONALD MACE WILLIAMS

Beowulf:
For Fireside and Schoolroom

The Nectar Dancer

Wolfe and Being Ninety:
Old West Monsters and a Texas Poet's Life

Interlude in Umbarger:
Italian POWs and a Texas Church

The Sparrow and the Hall

Black Tuesday's Child

Wolfe and Other Poems

Timberline, U.S.A.:
High-Country Encounters from California to Maine

POEMS BY

Rainer Maria Rilke
A 150TH ANNIVERSARY READER

TRANSLATIONS BY
Donald Mace Williams

FROM
The Hour Book, The Book of Pictures, New Poems,
and the Second Part of *New Poems* (1902-1908)

Copyright © 2025 by Donald Mace Williams

ISBN: 978-1-965766-34-7
ISBN (ebook): 978-1-965766-35-4
Library of Congress Control Number: 2025903566

All rights reserved. No part of this book may be reproduced
in any form or by any electronic or mechanical means,
including information storage and retrieval systems,
without written permission from the author,
except for the use of brief quotations in a book review
or certain other noncommercial uses
permitted by copyright law.

Cover and interior design by Vivian Freeman Chaffin

Author photo by Dagmar Grieder

Printed in the United States

Introduction

For much of his writing life, Rainer Maria Rilke (1875-1926) yearned for time and peace to write the long, great works that were taking form in his mind. When circumstances were finally right, those works, the *Duino Elegies,* did emerge. But before, after, and even amid their composition, Rilke also wrote many short lyric poems of remarkable beauty and intensity. To bring some of the best of those to English-speaking audiences is the purpose of this book.

Translating metrical verse metrically is hard going at best, and the difficulty is at least doubled in the case of these poems by the imaginative turns that Rilke gives to German words. I have struggled to find English equivalents of those turns. I have tried also, not always successfully, to match the rhymes, which in the original seem effortless. Often, rather than seem labored or to distort the basic sense of the words, I have had either to resort to slant rhyme, as Rilke scorned to do, or to skip any hint of rhyme.

But one thing I have not skipped and have seldom changed is the meter. To ignore the meter in translating, to my mind, is like ignoring the tune of a song. Rilke's short poems are unabashedly musical. I have tried to convey this character. If I have failed in this and in other respects, I hope that both you, the reader, and Rilke's shade will try to forgive me.

I am not a native speaker of German, and the grammar is far from my strong point. When I finished one of these translations (though never before) I always referred to at least one other translation as a double check. Edward Snow's prose translations in *The Poetry of Rilke* were vital for this purpose. Even after checking there or elsewhere, though, I let some errors pass. Dagmar Grieder, who was brought up in Germany, caught a number of those, saving me from certain embarrassment. I am very grateful to her, and neither she nor Edward Snow's book is responsible for errors that may remain.

—Donald Mace Williams

Contents

FROM **The Hour Book**
AUS **Das Stunden-Buch**

Untitled ["I live out my life"]   2
Ohne Titel ["Ich lebe mein Leben"]

Untitled ["I come upon you"]   3
Ohne Titel ["Ich finde dich"]

Untitled ["I am, you anxious man"]   4
Ohne Titel ["Ich bin, du Ängstlicher"]

Stanzas   5
Strophen

Untitled ["What will you do, God?"]   6
Ohne Titel ["Was wirst du tun, Herr?"]

Untitled ["Put out both eyes"]   8
Ohne Titel ["Lösch mir die Augen aus"]

Untitled ["Oh Lord, give us each"]   9
Ohne Titel ["O Herr, gib jedem"]

Untitled ["Perhaps in heavy mountains"]   10
Ohne Titel ["Vielleicht,
daß ich durch schwere Berge"]

Untitled ["My life is not"]   11
Ohne Titel ["Mein Leben ist nicht"]

Untitled ["In the deep nights"]   12
Ohne Titel ["In tiefen Nächten"]

Untitled ["Red barberries by now"]   14
Ohne Titel ["Jetz reifen schon"]

Untitled ["I am alive"]   15
Ohne Titel ["Ich lebe grad"]

FROM The Book of Pictures
AUS Das Buch der Bilder

Autumn Herbst	18
Evening Abend	19
Autumn Day Herbsttag	20
Entrance Eingang	21
Complaint Klage	22
The Angels Die Engel	24
The Toper's Song Das Lied des Trinkers	25
From a Childhood Aus einer Kindheit	26
A Recollection Erinnerung	27
The Orphan's Song Das Lied der Waise	28
At the Brink of Night Am Rande der Nacht	30
To Be Spoken at Bedtime Zum Einschlafen zu sagen	32
In Fear Bangnis	33
The Neighbor Der Nachbar	34

The Solitary Man Der Einsame	35
Bridge by the Carousel Pont du carrousel	36
Loneliness Einsamkeit	37
The Boy Der Knabe	38
From an April Aus einem April	40
Prayer Gebet	41
People at Night Menschen bei Nacht	42

FROM New Poems
AUS Neue Gedichte

The Panther Der Panther	46
The Last Evening Letzter Abend	47
Spanish Dancer Spanische Tänzerin	48
The Swan Der Schwan	50
Self Portrait from the Year 1906 Selbstbildnis aus dem Jahre 1906	51
Woman Going Blind Die Erblindende	52

The Girl Grown Up Die Erwachsene	54
A Woman's Fate Ein Frauenschicksal	56
Blue Hydrangea Blaue Hortensie	57
The Gazelle Die Gazelle	58
Love Song Liebes-Lied	60
Before the Summer Rain Vor dem Sommerregen	61
Death Experience Todes-Erfahrung	62
Roman Sarcophagi Römische Sarkophage	64
Departure Abschied	65
The Poet Der Dichter	66
The Donor Der Stifter	67
Saint Sebastian Sankt Sebastian	68
Buddha Buddha	69
The Carousel Das Karussell	70

FROM **New Poems, Second Part**
AUS **Neue Gedichte, Zweiter Teil**

Black Cat	74
Schwarze Katze	
A Wrinkled Woman	76
Eine Welke	
Archaic Torso of Apollo	77
Archäischer Torso Apollos	
Corpse-Washing	78
Leichen-Wäsche	
Piano Practice	80
Übung am Klavier	
Leda	81
Leda	
The Burned-Over Place	82
Die Brandstätte	
Lady on a Balcony	84
Dame auf einem Balkon	
Lady before the Mirror	85
Dame vor dem Spiegel	
The Sundial	86
Die Sonnenuhr	

FROM Uncollected Poems
AUS Nicht Eingesammelte Gedichte

The Loved One's Death — 90
Der Tod der Geliebten

Untitled ["Death is great"] — 91
Ohne Titel [Der Tod ist groß]

Untitled ["Workmen we are"] — 92
Ohne Titel ["Werkleute sind wir"]

Untitled ["That which the flying birds"] — 94
Ohne Titel ["Durch den sich Vögel werfen"]

Untitled ["Tears, tears that burst"] — 95
Ohne Titel ["Tränen, Tränen die aus mir brechen"]

Untitled ["Lifting my glance"] — 96
Ohne Titel ["Hebend die Blicke"]

Untitled ["We waken now"] — 97
Ohne Titel ["Nun wachen wir"]

Death — 98
Der Tod

Untitled ["Brother Body is poor"] — 100
Ohne Titel ["Bruder Körper ist arm"]

Untitled ["The bird calls are beginning"] — 101
Ohne Titel ["Die Vogelrufe fangen an"]

Full Power — 102
Vollmacht

Untitled ["Ah, loose in the wind"] — 103
Ohne Titel ["Ach, im Wind gelöst"]

Wild Rosebush — 104
Wilder Rosenbusch

Moonlit Night — 105
Mondnacht

The King of Munster Der König von Münster	106
Untitled ["That is yearning"] Ohne Titel ["Das ist die Sehnsucht"]	107
Untitled ["You come and go"] Ohne Titel ["Du kommst und gehst"]	108
Knight Ritter	110
End of Autumn Ende des Herbstes	112
The Deranged Ones Die Irren	113
Madness Der Wahnsinn	114
Sacrifice Opfer	116

FROM **The Sonnets to Orpheus**
AUS **Die Sonette an Orpheus**

Orpheus I, 1	118
Orpheus I, 7	120
Orpheus I, 9	121
Orpheus I, 14	122
Orpheus I, 15	123
Orpheus I, 18	124
Orpheus I, 19	125
Orpheus I, 21	126
Orpheus I, 24	127
Orpheus I, 25	128
Orpheus II, 2	129
Orpheus II, 4	130
Orpheus II, 6	131
Orpheus II, 20	132
Orpheus II, 23	133

FROM **The Hour Book**
AUS **Das Stunden-Buch**

Untitled ["I live out my life"]

I live out my life in widening rings
that extend over all below.
I may not make the last one a realized thing,
but intend to try doing so.

I circle God, circle the age-old tower,
and I circle millennia long;
and still do not know: am I hawk, thundershower,
or a magnificent song.

Ohne Titel ["Ich lebe mein Leben"]

Ich lebe mein Leben in wachsenden Ringen,
die sich über die Dinge ziehn.
Ich werde den letzten vielleicht nicht vollbringen,
aber versuchen will ich ihn.

Ich kreise um Gott, um den uralten Turm,
und ich kreise jahrtausendelang;
und ich weiß noch nicht: bin ich ein Falke, ein Sturm
oder ein großer Gesang.

Untitled ["I come upon you"]

I come upon you in all of these things
I love well and am like a brother to;
as seed you bask in trifles each day brings
and to great matters greatly give of you.

It is the wondrous game played out by strengths,
that they pass through all things so servingly,
grow in the root, dwindle all up the length,
then Resurrectionlike atop the tree.

Ohne Titel ["Ich finde dich"]

Ich finde dich in allen diesen Dingen,
denen ich gut und wie ein Bruder bin;
als Samen sonnst du dich in den geringen
und in den großen giebst du groß dich hin.

Das ist das wundersame Spiel der Kräfte,
dass sie so dienend durch die Dinge gehn:
in Wurzeln wachsend, schwindend in die Schäfte
und in den Wipfeln wie ein Auferstehn.

Untitled ["I am, you anxious man"]

I am, you anxious man. Do you not hear
me breaking over you with all my thought?
My feelings, which came on themselves winged-out,
circle your face whitely and near.
Do you not see my soul, how, densely sheer,
it stands dressed in a cloak of stillness there
in front of you? Does not my Maytime prayer
ripen upon your glance as on a tree?

If you shall be the dreamer, let me be
your dream. Your will, though, in your waking hours,
and in magnificence my powers climb
and grow whole like a stillness made of stars
hovering above the strange city of time.

Ohne Titel ["Ich bin, du Ängstlicher"]

Ich bin, du Ängstlicher. Hörst du mich nicht
mit allen meinen Sinnen an dir branden?
Meine Gefühle, welche Flügel fanden,
umkreisen weiß dein Angesicht.
Siehst du nicht meine Seele, wie sie dicht
vor dir in einem Kleid aus Stille steht?
Reift nicht mein mailiches Gebet
an deinem Blicke wie an einem Baum?

Wenn du der Träumer bist, bin ich dein Traum.
Doch wenn du wachen willst, bin ich dein Wille
und werde mächtig aller Herrlichkeit
und ründe mich wie eine Sternenstille
über der wunderlichen Stadt der Zeit.

Stanzas

One is, who those alive in his hand takes,
so sandlike they between his fingers run.
He chooses from the queens the fairest ones
and has them hewn out of the whitest marble,
still lying in the mantles' melody,
and lays kings there amid their ladies' number,
imagined from the very stone as they.

One is, who those alive in his hand takes,
that like bad blades they are and so they shatter.
He is no stranger, for he lives in blood,
which is our very life in calm and flood.
I cannot think he does a thing not good,
yet hear him charged with many an evil matter.

Strophen

Ist einer, der nimmt alle in die Hand,
daß sie wie Sand durch seine Finger rinnen.
Er wählt die schönsten aus den Königinnen
und läßt sie sich in weißen Marmor hauen,
still liegend in des Mantels Melodie;
und legt die Könige zu ihren Frauen,
gebildet aus dem gleichen Stein wie sie.

Ist einer, der nimmt alle in die Hand,
daß sie wie schlechte Klingen sind und brechen.
Er ist kein Fremder, denn er wohnt im Blut,
das unser Leben ist und rauscht und ruht.
Ich kann nicht glauben, daß er Unrecht tut;
doch hör ich viele Böses von ihm sprechen.

Untitled
["What will you do, God?"]

What will you do, God, when I die?
I am your urn (if in shards I fly?)
I am your quaff (if I turn wry?)
Am your robe, am the craft you ply.
With me, gone, too, your consciousness.

I gone, you have no house, the place
where intimate and warm words greet you.
From your two spent and weary feet, you
lose the plush sandals that are I.

Your massive overgarment drops.
Your gaze, for which I've always made
my pillowed cheek a welcome bed
will come, will seek me unallayed—
and lie at sunset's glowing shade
down in the lap of alien rocks.

What will you do, God? I'm afraid.

Ohne Titel
["Was wirst du tun"]

Was wirst du tun, Gott, wenn ich sterbe?
Ich bin dein Krug (wenn ich zerscherbe?)
Ich bin dein Trank (wenn ich verderbe?)
Bin dein Gewand und dein Gewerbe,
mit mir verlierst du deinen Sinn.

Nach mir hast du kein Haus, darin
dich Worte, nah und warm, begrüßen.
Es fällt von deinen müden Füßen
die Samtsandale, die ich bin.

Dein großer Mantel läßt dich los.
Dein Blick, den ich mit meiner Wange
warm, wie mit einem Pfühl, empfange,
wird kommen, wird mich suchen, lange—
und legt beim Sonnenuntergange
sich fremden Steinen in den Schoß.

Was wirst du tun, Gott? Ich bin bange.

Untitled ["Put out both eyes"]

Put out both eyes of mine: I still can see you,
shut down my two ears: I can hear you well,
and without feet I readily walk to you,
and without mouth I can beseech you still.
Break off my arms, I still contrive to grasp you
with just my heart, as if it were a hand,
squeeze my heart down, and yet my brain will pulse;
fling a hot coal into my brain,
then I will bear you up with just my blood.

Ohne Titel ["Lösch mir die Augen aus"]

Lösch mir die Augen aus: ich kann dich sehn,
wirf mir die Ohren zu: ich kann dich hören,
und ohne Füße kann ich zu dir gehn,
und ohne Mund noch kann ich dich beschwören.
Brich mir die Arme ab, ich fasse dich
mit meinem Herzen wie mit einer Hand,
halt mir das Herz zu, und mein Hirn wird schlagen,
und wirfst du in mein Hirn den Brand,
so werd ich dich auf meinem Blute tragen.

Untitled ["Oh Lord, give us each"]

Oh Lord, give us each his distinctive death.
A death that rises from that very life
in which he had love, thought, and troubled breath.

Ohne Titel ["O Herr, gib jedem"]

O Herr, gib jedem seinen eignen Tod.
Das Sterben, das aus jenem Leben geht,
darin er Liebe hatte, Sinn und Not.

Untitled ["Perhaps in heavy mountains"]

Perhaps in heavy mountains I walk here
through hardened veins like iron ore, alone;
and am so deep that no end light appears
nor any distance: all has turned to near
and all the near has turned to stone.

In ways of woe I am of course no seer,—
so this huge darkness makes me seem half-grown;
but if it's you: break through like heavy stone
so all your hand may lie upon me here
and I on you with all the cry I own.

Ohne Titel ["Vielleicht, daß ich durch schwere Berge"]

Vielleicht, daß ich durch schwere Berge gehe
in harten Adern, wie ein Erz allein;
und bin so tief, daß ich kein Ende sehe
und keine Ferne: alles wurde Nähe
und alle Nähe wurde Stein.

Ich bin ja noch kein Wissender im Wehe,—
so macht mich dieses große Dunkel klein;
bist Du es aber: mach dich schwer, brich ein:
daß deine ganze Hand an mir geschehe
und ich an dir mit meinem ganzen Schrein.

Untitled
["My life is not"]

My life is not this steeply rearing hour
in which you see me always rushed.
I am a tree before my own background,
I am just one among my many mouths
and that one that is earliest to shut.

I am the rest that makes a silent tether
between two notes which poorly come together:
for one note, death, sharps from below.

But in the dark of rest they meet each other,
both trembling.
                And the lovely song stays so.

Ohne Titel
["Mein Leben ist nicht"]

Mein Leben ist nicht diese steile Stunde,
darin du mich so eilen siehst.
Ich bin ein Baum vor meinem Hintergrunde,
ich bin nur einer meiner vielen Munde
und jener, welcher sich am frühsten schließt.

Ich bin die Ruhe zwischen zweien Tönen,
die sich nur schlecht aneinander gewöhnen:
denn der Ton Tod will sich erhöhn—

Aber im dunklen Intervall versöhnen
sich beide zitternd.
                Und das Lied bleibt schön.

Untitled ["In the deep nights"]

In the deep nights I dig for you, dear treasure.
For all the superfluities I've seen
are sorry substitutes, in wretched measure
to your great beauty, which has not yet been.

The road to you, though, stretches grimly far
and, long unused, is scattered by the winds.
You are alone—all solitude you are,
oh heart, that wanders to far-distant lands.

And both my hands, which from their shoveling
are bloody yet, aloft in air I bring,
hoping they will become branched like the trees.
With them, I draw you down from airy leas
as if you once had shattered yourself there
making a single gesture of impatience,
and fell now as a world of dusty air
from distant stars once more to earthly stations,
softly as springtime rains occur.

Ohne Titel ["In tiefen Nächten"]

In tiefen Nächten grab ich dich, du Schatz.
Denn alle Überflüsse, die ich sah,
sind Armut und armsäliger Ersatz
für deine Schönheit, die noch nie geschah.

Aber der Weg zu dir ist furchtbar weit
und, weil ihn lange keiner ging, verweht.
O du bist einsam. Du bist Einsamkeit,
du Herz, das zu entfernten Talen geht.

Und meine Hände, welche blutig sind
vom Graben, heb ich offen in den Wind,
so daß sie sich verzweigen wie ein Baum.
Ich sauge dich mit ihnen aus dem Raum
als hättest du dich einmal dort zerschellt
in einer ungeduldigen Gebärde,
und fielest jetzt, eine zerstäubte Welt,
aus fernen Sternen wieder auf die Erde
sanft wie ein Frühlingsregen fällt.

Untitled ["Red barberries assume"]

Red barberries assume now their ripe tone,
aging asters weakly breathe in their beds.
Whoever's not yet rich, as summer fades,
will wait forever and himself not own.

Whoever finds that his eyes will not shut—
of course, for in abundance, sights of old
wait in him only till the start of night,
so as to stand in his dark, which unfolds:—
that one, like an old man, has faded out.

Nothing more comes to him, no more days shine,
and all things that occur merely deceive him;
you too, my God. And you are like a stone
dragging him daily to the depths beneath him.

Ohne Titel ["Jetz reifen schon"]

Jetzt reifen schon die roten Berberitzen,
alternde Astern atmen schwach im Beet.
Wer jetzt nicht reich ist, da der Sommer geht,
wird immer warten und sich nie besitzen.

Wer jetzt nicht seine Augen schließen kann,
gewiß, daß eine Fülle von Gesichten
in ihm nur wartet bis die Nacht begann,
um sich in seinem Dunkel aufzurichten:—
der ist vergangen wie ein alter Mann.

Dem kommt nichts mehr, dem stößt kein Tag mehr zu,
und alles lügt ihn an, was ihm geschieht;
auch du, mein Gott. Und wie ein Stein bist du,
welcher ihn täglich in die Tiefe zieht.

Untitled ["I am alive"]

I am alive just as the century goes.
One feels the wind off a majestic page,
which God and you and I have written on
and which is turned, high up, in strangers' hands.

One feels the glow that comes from a new page,
on which all things can yet become.

The quiet powers make trial of their breadth
and fix their dark gaze on each other.

Ohne Titel ["Ich lebe grad"]

Ich lebe grad, da das Jahrhundert geht.
Man fühlt den Wind von einem großen Blatt,
das Gott und du und ich beschrieben hat
und das sich hoch in fremden Händen dreht.

Man fühlt den Glanz von einer neuen Seite,
auf der noch Alles werden kann.

Die stillen Kräfte prüfen ihre Breite
und sehn einander dunkel an.

FROM **The Book of Pictures**
AUS **Das Buch der Bilder**

Autumn

Leaves fall, they fall as from a distant place,
as if far gardens withered in the skies;
they fall with a denying attitude.

And in the nighttimes falls the heavy world
out of all stars into the solitude.

We all are falling. Falling, here, this hand.
And look at others: it is in them all.

Yet there exists One who all of this falling
forever softly holds within his hands.

Herbst

Die Blätter fallen, fallen wie von weit,
als welkten in den Himmeln ferne Gärten;
sie fallen mit verneinender Gebärde.

Und in den Nächten fällt die schwere Erde
aus allen Sternen in die Einsamkeit.

Wir alle fallen. Diese Hand da fällt.
Und sieh dir andre an: es ist in allen.

Und doch ist Einer, welcher dieses Fallen
unendlich sanft in seinen Händen hält.

Evening

The evening changes slowly now its garments,
held for it by the old woods' leafy wall;
you watch: and from you realms begin departing,
one heaven-traveler and one that falls;

and leave you, neither realm's complete adherent,
not fully darkened like the silent house,
not fully sure as witness to the eternal
like what each night becomes a star and rises;

and leave you (words cannot tell the untangling)
your life, maturing, huge, and full of fear,
so that it, now shut in, now seeing clearly,
is now a stone in you and now a star.

Abend

Der Abend wechselt langsam die Gewänder,
die ihm ein Rand von alten Bäumen hält;
du schaust: und von dir scheiden sich die Länder,
ein himmelfahrendes und eins, das fällt;

und lassen dich, zu keinem ganz gehörend,
nicht ganz so dunkel wie das Haus, das schweigt,
nicht ganz so sicher Ewiges beschwörend
wie das, was Stern wird jede Nacht und steigt;

und lassen dir (unsäglich zu entwirrn)
dein Leben bang und riesenhaft und reifend,
so daß es, bald begrenzt und bald begreifend,
abwechselnd Stein in dir wird und Gestirn.

Autumn Day

Lord: it is time. Summer was fine indeed.
Now lay your shadow on the sundials,
and on the meadows let the winds be freed.

Give the last fruits the order for completeness;
provide them two more south-begotten days,
urge them to their fulfilment, and then haze
into the heavy wine its final sweetness.

Whoever has no house, no house will build.
Whoever is alone shall long be so,
shall write long letters, read, and hardly go
to sleep, shall walk the byways, never stilled,
and wander without rest as last leaves blow.

Herbsttag

Herr: es ist Zeit. Der Sommer war sehr groß.
Leg deinen Schatten auf die Sonnenuhren,
und auf den Fluren laß die Winde los.

Befiehl den letzten Früchten voll zu sein;
gieb ihnen noch zwei südlichere Tage,
dränge sie zur Vollendung hin und jage
die letzte Süße in den schweren Wein.

Wer jetzt kein Haus hat, baut sich keines mehr.
Wer jetzt allein ist, wird es lange bleiben,
wird wachen, lesen, lange Briefe schreiben
und wird in den Alleen hin und her
unruhig wandern, wenn die Blätter treiben.

Entrance

Whoever you are: When evening comes, step out
of your room there, in which you know all things;
just before the distance lies your house:
whoever you are.
And with your tired eyes, which can barely free
themselves from the much-trodden threshold there,
you gradually raise up a black tree
and place it near to heaven: alone and spare.
And you have made the world. And it is huge,
and like a word that in the hush ripes on.
And as your purpose comprehends its mind,
your eyes with gentle love shall set it loose…

Eingang

Wer du auch seist: Am Abend tritt hinaus
aus deiner Stube, drin du alles weißt;
als letztes vor der Ferne liegt dein Haus:
wer du auch seist.
Mit deinen Augen, welche müde kaum
von der verbrauchten Schwelle sich befrein,
hebst du ganz langsam einen schwarzen Baum
und stellst ihn vor den Himmel: schlank, allein.
Und hast die Welt gemacht. Und sie ist groß
und wie ein Wort, das noch im Schweigen reift.
Und wie dein Wille ihren Sinn begreift,
lassen sie deine Augen zärtlich los…

Complaint

How all things are afar
and long since faded.
I think the one star
with whose light I am pervaded
died millenniums ago.
I think in the boat
that just passed by
I heard a fearsome thought propounded.
In the house the time
has sounded…
In what house?…
I wish to step from my heart and go out
underneath the mighty heavens' array.
I wish to pray.
And one among the stars
must really still exist.
I think I would know
which lone one is this
that has survived—
which like a city all in white
stands in the heavens at the end of its beam…

Klage

O wie ist alles fern
und lange vergangen.
Ich glaube, der Stern,
von welchem ich Glanz empfange,
ist seit Jahrtausenden tot.
Ich glaube, im Boot,
das vorüberfuhr,
hörte ich etwas Banges sagen.
Im Hause hat eine Uhr
geschlagen...
In welchem Haus?...
Ich möchte aus meinem Herzen hinaus
unter den großen Himmel treten.
Ich möchte beten.
Und einer von allen Sternen
müßte wirklich noch sein.
Ich glaube, ich wüßte,
welcher allein
gedauert hat,—
welcher wie eine weiße Stadt
am Ende des Strahls in den Himmeln steht...

The Angels

They every one have weary mouths
and their bright souls are without seams.
And sometimes yearning (as for sin)
finds its own passage through their dreams.

Each one looks almost like the next;
in God's high gardens they stand mute
like many and many a long-held rest
in his great melody and might.

Only when they spread their wings
are they the stirrers of a wind:
As if God, with his sculptor's fingers,
broad-handed riffled through dark leaves
of the book wherein all things begin.

Die Engel

Sie haben alle müde Münde
und helle Seelen ohne Saum.
Und eine Sehnsucht (wie nach Sünde)
geht ihnen manchmal durch den Traum.

Fast gleichen sie einander alle;
in Gottes Gärten schweigen sie,
wie viele, viele Intervalle
in seiner Macht und Melodie.

Nur wenn sie ihre Flügel breiten,
sind sie die Wecker eines Winds:
als ginge Gott mit seinen weiten
Bildhauerhänden durch die Seiten
im dunklen Buch des Anbeginns.

The Toper's Song

It was not in me. It went out and in.
I wanted to hold it. What held it was wine.
(I no longer know what it was.)
Wine offered me that and offered me this
till I was no longer mine, just its:
An ass.

Now I am into its game and it strews
me about with contempt, so as to lose
me to this beast, to this death.
When I, soiled card, come up in death's draw,
he scratches his gray poll with me in his paw,
and tosses me out in the filth.

Das Lied des Trinkers

Es war nicht in mir. Es ging aus und ein.
Da wollt ich es halten. Da hielt es der Wein.
(Ich weiß nicht mehr was es war.)
Dann hielt er mir jenes und hielt mir dies
bis ich mich ganz auf ihn verließ.
Ich Narr.

Jetzt bin ich in seinem Spiel und er streut
mich verächtlich herum und verliert mich noch heut
an dieses Vieh, an den Tod.
Wenn der mich, schmutzige Karte, gewinnt,
so kratzt er mit mir seinen grauen Grind
und wirft mich fort in den Kot.

From a Childhood

Darkness was like riches in the room
in which the boy, concealed indeed, was sitting.
And when the mother came, as in a dream,
a glass on a still shelf was heard to quiver.
She felt as by the room itself betrayed
and then she kissed her youngster: Are you here?...
They both, then, looked in fright at the clavier,
since many evenings there was a song she played
in which the child felt strangely, deeply snared.

He sat quite still. Intently now he stared
at her hand, which, by the ring sharply bent,
as if its way through snowdrifts went,
passed over the ivory-white keyboard.

Aus einer Kindheit

Das Dunkeln war wie Reichtum in dem Raume,
darin der Knabe, sehr verheimlicht, saß.
Und als die Mutter eintrat wie im Traume,
erzitterte im stillen Schrank ein Glas.
Sie fühlte, wie das Zimmer sie verriet,
und küßte ihren Knaben: Bist du hier?...
Dann schauten beide bang nach dem Klavier,
denn manchen Abend hatte sie ein Lied,
darin das Kind sich seltsam tief verfing.

Es saß sehr still. Sein großes Schauen hing
an ihrer Hand, die ganz gebeugt vom Ringe,
als ob sie schwer in Schneewehn ginge,
über die weißen Tasten ging.

A Recollection

And you wait, you wait for the one
that unceasingly broadens your being;
the mighty, the likened to none,
the awakening of stones,
of depth brought forth for your seeing.

In the bookcase, light grows dim
on volumes of brown and gold;
and you think of lands you have seen,
of pictures, and clothes once again
of women lost of old.

And you suddenly know: It was that.
You get up, and before you, there,
there stands, of a year in the past,
the fear and form and prayer.

Erinnerung

Und du wartest, erwartest das Eine,
das dein Leben unendlich vermehrt;
das Mächtige, Ungemeine,
das Erwachen der Steine,
Tiefen, dir zugekehrt.

Es dämmern im Bücherständer
die Bände in Gold und Braun;
und du denkst an durchfahrene Länder,
an Bilder, an die Gewänder
wiederverlorener Fraun.

Und da weißt du auf einmal: Das war es.
Du erhebst dich, und vor dir steht
eines vergangenen Jahres
Angst und Gestalt und Gebet.

The Orphan's Song

I am No one and No one I shall be.
As yet I am too small for being;
later, not other.

Fathers and mothers,
have pity on me.

Caring for me is not worth the time:
I get mown, just the same.
No one has need of me: now is too soon,
and tomorrow will be too late.

There is just this single dress for me,
it is fading and thinning out
but it will last an eternity
before God, I have little doubt.

I have only this bit of hair
(it always stays the same)
that belonged to a certain someone dear.

Nothing has stayed dear to him.

Das Lied der Waise

Ich bin Niemand und werde auch Niemand sein.
Jetzt bin ich ja zum Sein noch zu klein;
aber auch später.

Mütter und Väter,
erbarmt euch mein.

Zwar es lohnt nicht des Pflegens Müh:
ich werde doch gemäht.
Mich kann keiner brauchen: jetzt ist es zu früh,
und morgen ist es zu spät.

Ich habe nur dieses eine Kleid,
es wird dünn und es verbleicht,
aber es hält eine Ewigkeit
auch noch vor Gott vielleicht.

Ich habe nur dieses bißchen Haar
(immer dasselbe blieb),
dass einmal Eines Liebstes war.

Nun hat er nichts mehr lieb.

At the Brink of Night

My room and this vast thing,
wakeful over the repetitious land,
are one. I am a violin string
stretched above the clamoring
resonances' expanse.

Things are violins' bodies,
full of a grumbling shade;
there women's weeping dreams,
there the rancor of ages is laid,
stirring in sleep.

I shall
silverly vibrate: all must,
beneath me, then live,
and what in things has lost
its way will strive toward the light
that from my dancing sound,
to which the heavens pulse,
through tiny, languishing slits
in the old
abysses, without
end falls...

Am Rande der Nacht

Meine Stube und diese Weite,
wach über nachbetendem Land,—
ist Eines. Ich bin eine Saite,
über rauschende breite
Resonanzen gespannt.

Die Dinge sind Geigenleiber,
von murrendem Dunkel voll;
drin träumt das Weinen der Weiber,
drin rührt sich im Schlafe der Groll
ganzer Geschlechter…

Ich soll
silbern erzittern: dann wird
Alles unter mir leben,
und was in den Dingen irrt,
wird nach dem Lichte streben,
das von meinem tanzenden Tone,
um welchen der Himmel wellt,
durch schmale, schmachtende Spalten
in die alten
Abgründe ohne
Ende fällt…

To Be Spoken at Bedtime

I wish I could lullaby someone,
with someone sit and be;
could rock you, croon you a song, or hum one
and be with you awake and asleep.
I wish I could be, in the house, the one
who knew this: the night was cold.
I'd like to listen, going or coming on,
to you, to the woods, to the world.
The clocks hail each other, strike once and again,
and we look upon time's very ground.
Below, there keeps walking an unknown man
and stirs up an unknown hound.
Behind that comes quiet. I've turned my eyes,
expansive, onto your form;
and softly they hold you, and let you loose
if a Thing moves about in the dark.

Zum Einschlafen zu sagen

Ich möchte jemanden einsingen,
bei jemandem sitzen und sein.
Ich möchte dich wiegen und kleinsingen
und begleiten schlafaus und schlafein.
Ich möchte der Einzige sein im Haus,
der wüßte: die Nacht war kalt.
Und möchte horchen herein und hinaus
in dich, in die Welt, in den Wald.
Die Uhren rufen sich schlagend an,
und man sieht der Zeit auf den Grund.
Und unten geht noch ein fremder Mann
und stört einen fremden Hund.
Dahinter wird Stille. Ich habe groß
die Augen auf dich gelegt;
und sie halten dich sanft und lassen dich los,
wenn ein Ding sich im Dunkel bewegt.

In Fear

In withered woods there sounds out a bird call,
which seems without sense in these withered woods.
And nonetheless, the simple, clear bird call
rests in this bit of time, which made it,
broad as a sky over the withered woods.
Compliant, at the cry all things make room:
the whole land seems at rest and without sound,
the great wind seems to nestle still around,
even the moment, which wants to move on,
is pale and hushed, as if it could descry
the things by which each man must die,
from it arisen unbound.

Bangnis

Im welken Walde ist ein Vogelruf,
der sinnlos scheint in diesem welken Walde.
Und dennoch ruht der runde Vogelruf
in dieser Weile, die ihn schuf,
breit wie ein Himmel auf dem welken Walde.
Gefügig räumt sich alles in den Schrei:
Das ganze Land scheint lautlos drin zu liegen,
der große Wind scheint sich hineinzuschmiegen,
und die Minute, welche weiter will,
ist bleich und still, als ob sie Dinge wüßte,
an denen jeder sterben müßte,
aus ihm herausgestiegen.

The Neighbor

Violin, stranger, are you following me?
How many distant cities must there be
where your lonely night spoke to mine?
Do hundreds play you? Does just one?

In all great cities do there reside
such as, if they did not have you,
would have lost themselves in the tide?
Why always with me does it have to do?

Why am I always being the neighbor
of those who in terror make you sing
and declare: our life is heavier
than the weight of all earth's things.

Der Nachbar

Fremde Geige, gehst du mir nach?
In wieviel fernen Städten schon sprach
deine einsame Nacht zu meiner?
Spielen dich hunderte? Spielt dich einer?

Giebt es in allen großen Städten
solche, die sich ohne dich
schon in den Flüssen verloren hätten?
Und warum trifft es immer mich?

Warum bin ich immer der Nachbar derer,
die dich bange zwingen zu singen
und zu sagen: Das Leben ist schwerer
als die Schwere von allen Dingen.

The Solitary Man

Like one who has roamed into alien seas,
so am I when with natives of a place;
their tables are the scenes of filled-up days,
I, though, see only distant mysteries.

A world, come to my eyes to be reflected,
may be unpopulated like a moon,
but they can let no feeling lie neglected,
and every word of theirs is lived upon.

The things I chose from far to stay with me,
held up against their things, seldom look out—:
in their large realm, like beasts they move about,
here they hold tight their breath in modesty.

Der Einsame

Wie einer, der auf fremden Meeren fuhr,
so bin ich bei den ewig Einheimischen;
die vollen Tage stehn auf ihren Tischen,
mir aber ist die Ferne voll Figur.

In mein Gesicht reicht eine Welt herein,
die vielleicht unbewohnt ist wie ein Mond,
sie aber lassen kein Gefühl allein,
und alle ihre Worte sind bewohnt.

Die Dinge, die ich weither mit mir nahm,
sehn selten aus, gehalten an das Ihre—:
in ihrer großen Heimat sind sie Tiere,
hier halten sie den Atem an vor Scham.

Bridge by the Carousel

The blind man who is standing on the bridge,
gray like a boundary stone of nameless lands,
perhaps he is the thing that always stands,
by which, from far away, star time is fixed,
and is the constellations' quiet center.
For all around him flows and strays and glitters.

He is the righteous one, immovable,
set down on many a snarled, chaotic road;
the dismal entrance to the underworld
amid a race bent on the trivial.

Pont du carrousel

Der blinde Mann, der auf der Brücke steht,
grau wie ein Markstein namenloser Reiche,
er ist vielleicht das Ding, das immer gleiche,
um das von fern die Sternenstunde geht,
und der Gestirne stiller Mittelpunkt.
Denn alles um ihn irrt und rinnt und prunkt.

Er ist der unbewegliche Gerechte,
in viele wirre Wege hingestellt;
der dunkle Eingang in die Unterwelt
bei einem oberflächlichen Geschlechte.

Loneliness

Loneliness is like a rain.
It rises toward the evenings from the sea;
from plains, which are remote and far away,
it goes to sky, where it is always found.
And only from the sky falls on the town.

Below it rains in the ambiguous hours
when morningward all lanes and alleys veer
and when the bodies, nothing having found,
hopeless and sad, part from each other here;
and those who hold each other in hate or fear
yet in the same bed have to sleep together:

then loneliness flows with the rivers…

Einsamkeit

Die Einsamkeit ist wie ein Regen.
Sie steigt vom Meer den Abenden entgegen;
von Ebenen, die fern sind und entlegen,
geht sie zum Himmel, der sie immer hat.
Und erst vom Himmel fällt sie auf die Stadt.

Regnet hernieder in den Zwitterstunden,
wenn sich nach Morgen wenden alle Gassen
und wenn die Leiber, welche nichts gefunden,
enttäuscht und traurig von einander lassen;
und wenn die Menschen, die einander hassen,
in *einem* Bett zusammen schlafen müssen:

dann geht die Einsamkeit mit den Flüssen…

The Boy

I would like to develop into one
like those who with wild horses drive through night
with torches, which like hair loose as in flight
wave in the mighty wind raised by their hunt.
I would stand forward as if in a boat,
as huge a presence as a flag unrolled.
Dark, but beneath a helmet made of gold
that casts light restlessly. And ranked behind,
ten men out of a darkness deep as mine
with helmets that, like mine, are always changing,
now clear as glass, now dark, or blind, or aging.
And one beside me stands and blows us room
upon a trumpet, which gleams and sounds out
and blows us a black loneness all about,
through which we rampage like a furious dream:
Behind us, houses fall onto their knees,
the streets and alleys bow their solid forms,
the market squares yield: we take hold of these,
and our wild horses pelt on like rain storms.

Der Knabe

Ich möchte einer werden so wie die,
die durch die Nacht mit wilden Pferden fahren,
mit Fackeln, die gleich aufgegangnen Haaren
in ihres Jagens großem Winde wehn.
Vorn möcht ich stehen wie in einem Kahne,
groß und wie eine Fahne aufgerollt.
Dunkel, aber mit einem Helm von Gold,
der unruhig glänzt. Und hinter mir gereiht
zehn Männer aus derselben Dunkelheit
mit Helmen, die, wie meiner, unstät sind,
bald klar wie Glas, bald dunkel, alt und blind.
Und einer steht bei mir und bläst uns Raum
mit der Trompete, welche blitzt und schreit,
und bläst uns eine schwarze Einsamkeit,
durch die wir rasen wie ein rascher Traum:
Die Häuser fallen hinter uns ins Knie,
die Gassen biegen sich uns schief entgegen,
die Plätze weichen aus: wir fassen sie,
und unsre Rosse rauschen wie ein Regen.

From an April

        The woods are fragrant again.
    The hovering larks lift with them
upward the heavens, of which our shoulders, before, felt the heft;
indeed we saw, through the branches, the nothing the day had left,—
    but after drawn-out and rain-filled afternoons
      here come the golden, sun-glistened
        new hours among us,
  before which fleeing, in housefronts off in the distance,
        fearful, the windows
    flap their loose wings as if from wounds.

Then all is still. Even the rain quiets now
onto the stones' calmly darkening glow.
All sounds without reserve let themselves go
into the soft-glowing buds of the bough.

Aus einem April

        Wieder duftet der Wald.
    Es heben die schwebenden Lerchen
mit sich den Himmel empor, der unseren Schultern schwer war;
zwar sah man noch durch die Äste den Tag, wie er leer war,—
    aber nach langen, regnenden Nachmittagen
      kommen die goldübersonnten
        neueren Stunden,
    vor denen flüchtend an fernen Häuserfronten
        alle die wunden
    Fenster furchtsam mit Flügeln schlagen.

Dann wird es still. Sogar der Regen geht leiser
über der Steine ruhig dunkelnden Glanz.
Alle Geräusche ducken sich ganz
in die glänzenden Knospen der Reiser.

Prayer

Night, silent night, in which are interwoven
all-white things, red, and many-colored things,
scattered-out colors that are lifted over
into one darkness of one silence,—bring
me into understanding with the many
you have persuaded and acquired. Do any
of my sensations play too much with light?
Will my face then, beset with doubt
by circumstance, stand out in clarity?
Judge by my hands: Do they not seem to be,
lying together, useful tool and thing?
Is not their ring also
all plainness, and does light not glow
just so, upon them, in full confidence,—
as if they might be roads, which in its glance
not differently branch out than in the dark?...

Gebet

Nacht, stille Nacht, in die verwoben sind
ganz weiße Dinge, rote, bunte Dinge,
verstreute Farben, die erhoben sind
zu Einem Dunkel Einer Stille,—bringe
doch mich auch in Beziehung zu dem Vielen,
das du erwirbst und überredest. Spielen
denn meine Sinne noch zu sehr mit Licht?
Würde sich denn mein Angesicht
noch immer störend von den Gegenständen
abheben? Urteile nach meinen Händen:
Liegen sie nicht wie Werkzeug da und Ding?
Ist nicht der Ring selbst schlicht
an meiner Hand, und liegt das Licht
nicht ganz so, voll Vertrauen, über ihnen,—
als ob sie Wege wären, die, beschienen,
nicht anders sich verzweigen, als im Dunkel?...

People at Night

Nights are in no sense fashioned for all.
They cut off your neighbor from you like a wall
with a barrier you never should try to undo.
And if at dark you turn up your light
in hope of a face-to-face human sight,
you have to consider: who.

Light has most horribly altered men's faces,
as from their features the evidence drips,
and if they go, nights, to gathering places,
you see there a world on a teetering basis
strewn as random as chips.
On all the foreheads a yellow shine
has taken the place of thought,
in their expressions is flickering wine,
and in their hands is caught
a ponderous gesture, with which they try
to make what they say clear and clever;
and therein reiterate *I* and *I*
which is to say: whoever.

Menschen bei Nacht

Die Nächte sind nicht für die Menge gemacht.
Von deinem Nachbar trennt dich die Nacht,
und du sollst ihn nicht suchen trotzdem.
Und machst du nachts deine Stube licht,
um Menschen zu schauen ins Angesicht,
so mußt du bedenken: wem.

Die Menschen sind furchtbar vom Licht entstellt,
das von ihren Gesichtern träuft,
und haben sie nachts sich zusammengesellt,
so schaust du eine wankende Welt
durcheinander gehäuft.
Auf ihren Stirnen hat gelber Schein
alle Gedanken verdrängt,
in ihren Blicken flackert der Wein,
an ihren Händen hängt
die schwere Gebärde, mit der sie sich
bei ihren Gesprächen verstehn;
und dabei sagen sie: *Ich* und *Ich*
und meinen: Irgendwen.

FROM **New Poems**
AUS **Neue Gedichte**

The Panther

From so much watching of the bars, at last
his weary eyes have surfeited and dulled.
A thousand bars, it seems to him, have passed,
a thousand, and behind the bars no world.

His padded course of strong and supple strides,
turning always in this restrictive round,
is like a dance that powerfully rides
around a mighty will, numbed and profound.

Rarely the curtain of his eyes does rise,
without a sound.—An image enters then,
moves through the silent tension of his thighs—
and in his heart fades out again.

Der Panther

Sein Blick ist vom Vorübergehn der Stäbe
so müd geworden, daß er nichts mehr hält.
Ihm ist, als ob es tausend Stäbe gäbe
und hinter tausend Stäben keine Welt.

Der weiche Gang geschmeidig starker Schritte,
der sich im allerkleinsten Kreise dreht,
ist wie ein Tanz von Kraft um eine Mitte,
in der betäubt ein großer Wille steht.

Nur manchmal schiebt der Vorhang der Pupille
sich lautlos auf.—Dann geht ein Bild hinein,
geht durch der Glieder angespannte Stille—
und hört im Herzen auf zu sein.

The Last Evening

And night, and distant movement; for in squads
the army, massed, was passing by that place.
He raised his eyes, though, from the harpsichord,
and playing on, looked over at her face

almost like looking in a mirror: fraught
so much with his own youthful countenance,
and knew that image bore his sadness thence
comely and more beguiling with each note.

But suddenly all this seemed to have blurred:
struggling within the window-niche she stood
and bore the urgent pounding of her heart.

His music stopped. A breeze from outside stirred.
And on the mirror table, alien, weird,
the tall black shako with its death's-head sat.

Letzter Abend

Und Nacht und fernes Fahren; denn der Train
des ganzen Heeres zog am Park vorüber.
Er aber hob den Blick vom Clavecin
und spielte noch und sah zu ihr hinüber

beinah, wie man in einen Spiegel schaut:
so sehr erfüllt von seinen jungen Zügen
und wissend, wie sie seine Trauer trügen,
schön und verführender bei jedem Laut.

Doch plötzlich wars, als ob sich das verwische:
sie stand wie mühsam in der Fensternische
und hielt des Herzens drängendes Geklopf.

Sein Spiel gab nach. Von draußen wehte Frische.
Und seltsam fremd stand auf dem Spiegeltische
der schwarze Tschako mit dem Totenkopf.

Spanish Dancer

As, in the hand, a sulphur match, pale, sends
before flame comes, outward to every side
quickly pulsating tonguelets—: now begins,
bright, burning, brisk for the ringed audience
her circled dance, pulsing, to fling out wide.

And suddenly it has become pure fire.

With a mere glance she kindles now her hair
and all at once draws with an artist's daring
her whole costume into the scarlet flaring,
from which, like horrifying snakes, her arms
thrust out their bare, alert, and clattering forms.

And then: as if the fire were too tight-fit,
she gathers it together and casts it,
all haughty, with a lofty gesture, down
and looks: it lies there raging on the ground
and keeps on flaming, will not yield to die—.
But she gives, sure in victory, a sweet
intimate smile, and, turning up her eye,
stamps out the fire with little firm-set feet.

Spanische Tänzerin

Wie in der Hand ein Schwefelzündholz, weiß,
eh es zur Flamme kommt, nach allen Seiten
zuckende Zungen streckt—: beginnt im Kreis
naher Beschauer hastig, hell und heiß
ihr runder Tanz sich zuckend auszubreiten.

Und plötzlich ist er Flamme, ganz und gar.

Mit einem Blick enzündet sie ihr Haar
und dreht auf einmal mit gewagter Kunst
ihr ganzes Kleid in diese Feuersbrunst,
aus welcher sich, wie Schlangen die erschrecken,
die nackten Arme wach und klappernd strecken.

Und dann: als würde ihr das Feuer knapp,
nimmt sie es ganz zusamm und wirft es ab
sehr herrisch, mit hochmütiger Gebärde
und schaut: da liegt es rasend auf der Erde
und flammt noch immer und ergiebt sich nicht—:
Doch sieghaft, sicher und mit einem süßen
grüßenden Lächeln hebt sie ihr Gesicht
und stampft es aus mit kleinen festen Füßen.

The Swan

This toil, going through the not-yet-done
heavily, as if with ankles bound,
is like the never-mastered walk of the swan.

And death, this no more being able to sense
that which we daily stand upon, the ground,
is like his anxious landing at flight's end—:

in waters, which with softness take him on
and, as if happy, as if all were done,
stream backward under him in flood on flood,
while he, forever silent and secure,
more and more kingly, more and more mature
and calmer, deigns to take his watery road.

Der Schwan

Diese Mühsal, durch noch Ungetanes
schwer and wie gebunden hinzugehn,
gleicht dem ungeschaffnen Gang des Schwanes.

Und das Sterben, dieses Nichtmehrfassen
jenes Grunds, auf dem wir täglich stehn,
seinem ängstlichen Sich-Niederlassen—:

in die Wasser, die ihn sanft empfangen
und die sich, wie glücklich und vergangen,
unter ihm zurückziehn, Flut um Flut;
während er unendlich still und sicher
immer mündiger und königlicher
und gelassener zu ziehn geruht.

Self Portrait from the Year 1906

Steadfastness of a longtime noble line
in the construction of the arched eyebrow.
In the gaze, childhood's anxiety and blue,
humility too, not the menial kind
but helpful and of such as women know.
The mouth made as mouth is, large, formed just-so,
not a persuasive one but with a fine
assertiveness. The forehead with no sign
of malice, glad of shade from head turned low.

All that, as unity faintly perceived;
neither in sorrow nor yet in success
formed in a lasting and emphatic stress
but as if, from far things picked with randomness,
an earnest, genuine thing had been conceived.

Selbstbildnis aus dem Jahre 1906

Des alten lange adligen Geschlechtes
Feststehendes im Augenbogenbau.
Im Blicke noch der Kindheit Angst und Blau
und Demut da und dort, nicht eines Knechtes
doch eines Dienenden und einer Frau.
Der Mund als Mund gemacht, groß und genau,
nicht überredend, aber ein Gerechtes
Aussagendes. Die Stirne ohne Schlechtes
und gern im Schatten stiller Niederschau.

Das, als Zusammenhang, erst nur geahnt;
noch nie im Leiden oder im Gelingen
zusammgefaßt zu dauerndem Durchdringen,
doch so, als wäre mit zerstreuten Dingen
von fern ein Ernstes, Wirkliches geplant.

Woman Going Blind

She sat at tea like others, guests and host.
The way she held her cup, it soon struck me,
was a bit different from the others' way.
She smiled a little once. It hurt, almost.

And when they stood up, talking, finally,
and slowly and as if by mere chance walked
away through many rooms (they laughed and talked),
I saw her. She was walking in their lee,

contained, much like one on her way to take
the stage and sing in front of a large crowd;
her bright eyes, in which a deep pleasure showed,
reflected light from outward, like a lake.

She followed slowly, as if something more
remained to be stepped over by and by;
but also: as if, once beyond that door,
she did not plan to walk then, but to fly.

Die Erblindende

Sie saß so wie die anderen beim Tee.
Mir war zuerst, als ob sie ihre Tasse
ein wenig anders als die andern fasse.
Sie lächelte einmal. Es tat fast weh.

Und als man schließlich sich erhob und sprach
und langsam und wie es der Zufall brachte
durch viele Zimmer ging (man sprach und lachte),
da sah ich sie. Sie ging den andern nach,

verhalten, so wie eine, welche gleich
wird singen müssen und vor vielen Leuten;
auf ihren hellen Augen die sich freuten
war Licht von außen wie auf einem Teich.

Sie folgte langsam und sie brauchte lang
als wäre etwas noch nicht überstiegen;
und doch: als ob, nach einem Übergang,
sie nicht mehr gehen würde, sondern fliegen.

The Girl Grown Up

It all rested on her and was the world
and stood on her with all, mercy and fright,
as trees stand, growing and always forthright,
all form and formless like the Ark of Light
and festive, like a leader just installed.

And she endured it; carried easily
the flying, fleeing, the grown-far-away,
the huge, the not-yet-learned-so-as-to-stay,
calm as the water girl who casually
bears the full jug. Till midway of the game,
still changing and with plans not yet full-grown,
the first white veil dropped, gliding softly down
until across her open face it came

almost opaque and nevermore to rise
and somehow to all things she wished to know
saying with vagueness that one answer lies:
In you, you child that was before, in you.

Die Erwachsene

Das alles stand auf ihr und war die Welt
und stand auf ihr mit allem, Angst und Gnade,
wie Bäume stehen, wachsend und gerade,
ganz Bild und bildlos wie die Bundeslade
und feierlich, wie auf ein Volk gestellt.

Und sie ertrug es; trug bis obenhin
das Fliegende, Entfliehende, Entfernte,
das Ungeheuere, noch Unerlernte
gelassen wie die Wasserträgerin
den vollen Krug. Bis mitten unterm Spiel,
verwandelnd und auf andres vorbereitend,
der erste weiße Schleier, leise gleitend,
über das aufgetane Antlitz fiel

fast undurchsichtig und sich nie mehr hebend
und irgendwie auf alle Fragen ihr
nur eine Antwort vage wiedergebend:
In dir, du Kindgewesene, in dir.

A Woman's Fate

Just as the king, out hunting, takes a glass,
a random one, so he can quench his thirst—
and as, thereafter, he whose glass it was
puts it away to keep, a matter of course:

so, possibly, a thirsty Fate one day
lifted a Woman to its mouth and drank,
and then a petty life, even as he shrank
from breaking her, her usefulness passé,

put her into a case, its care well shown,
in which his costly objects could be found
(the ones, at least, that passed for costly there).

She stood then, foreign, like a thing on loan,
simply becoming old and simply blind
and was not costly and was never rare.

Ein Frauenschicksal

So wie der König auf der Jagd ein Glas
ergreift, daraus zu trinken, irgendeines,—
und wie hernach der, welcher es besaß,
es fortstellt und verwahrt, als wär es keines:

so hob vielleicht das Schicksal, durstig auch,
bisweilen Eine an den Mund und trank,
die dann ein kleines Leben, viel zu bang
sie zu zerbrechen, abseits vom Gebrauch

hinstellte in die ängstliche Vitrine,
in welcher seine Kostbarkeiten sind
(oder die Dinge, die für kostbar gelten).

Da stand sie fremd wie eine Fortgeliehne
und wurde einfach alt und wurde blind
und war nicht kostbar und war niemals selten.

Blue Hydrangea

Much like, in crucibles, a final green,
these leaves appear, wrinkled, dull, and dried out,
behind the blossom-umbels, which do not
wear blue, only its far-off, mirrored sheen.

They mirror it tear-stained and inexact
as if they wished to lose it once again,
and as in old, blue stationery then
is yellow there, and gray, and violet;

washed-out as with a little children's shirtwaist,
a no-longer-worn one, now put away:
how one is struck here with a small life's shortness.

But suddenly the blue is once more seen
in one of the umbels, which now displays
a poignant blueness happy in the green.

Blaue Hortensie

So wie das letzte Grün in Farbentiegeln
sind diese Blätter, trocken, stumpf und rauh,
hinter den Blütendolden, die ein Blau
nicht auf sich tragen, nur von ferne spiegeln.

Sie spiegeln es verweint und ungenau,
als wollten sie es wiederum verlieren,
und wie in alten blauen Briefpapieren
ist Gelb in ihnen, Violett und Grau;

Verwaschnes wie an einer Kinderschürze,
Nichtmehrgetragnes, dem nichts mehr geschieht:
wie fühlt man eines kleinen Lebens Kürze.

Doch plötzlich scheint das Blau sich zu verneuen
in einer von den Dolden, und man sieht
ein rührend Blaues sich vor Grünem freuen.

The Gazelle

Gazella Dorcas

Bewitched one: how can two selected words
in their concord ever achieve the rhyme
that in you comes and goes as at a sign.
Up from your forehead leaf and lyre ascend,

and your whole being moves as simile
as if through love songs, those whose lyrics lie
like rose leaves softly on the eyes of him
who having stopped his reading closes them:

so he can see you: carried off, as though
each of your movements were somehow spring-laden
and might not shoot away while your neck so

holds your head harkening: like her who bathes
deep in the woods, whose bath is broken off:
the pond in her aside-turned countenance.

Die Gazelle

Gazella Dorcas

Verzauberte: wie kann der Einklang zweier
erwählter Worte je den Reim erreichen,
der in dir kommt und geht, wie auf ein Zeichen.
Aus deiner Stirne steigen Laub und Leier,

und alles Deine geht schon im Vergleich
durch Liebeslieder, deren Worte, weich
wie Rosenblätter, dem, der nicht mehr liest,
sich auf die Augen legen, die er schließt:

um dich zu sehen: hingetragen, als
wäre mit Sprüngen jeder Lauf geladen
und schöße nur nicht ab, solang der Hals

das Haupt im Horchen hält: wie wenn beim Baden
im Wald die Badende sich unterbricht:
den Waldsee im gewendeten Gesicht.

Love Song

How shall I keep my soul here, motionless,
so that it does not touch your own? How shall
I lift it over you to other things?
Oh! I should like to house it in some place
lost in the blackest dark that nightfall brings,
within an alien setting, one so still
its swinging holds off while your great depths swing.
But everything that troubles you and me
brings us together like a bow drawn free,
so from two strings a single voice is born.
Across what instrument have we been spanned?
What violinist has us in the hand?
O sweetest song!

Liebes-Lied

Wie soll ich meine Seele halten, daß
sie nicht an deine rührt? Wie soll ich sie
hinheben über dich zu andern Dingen?
Ach gerne möcht ich sie bei irgendwas
Verlorenem im Dunkel unterbringen
an einer fremden stillen Stelle, die
nicht weiterschwingt, wenn deine Tiefen schwingen.
Doch alles, was uns anrührt, dich und mich,
nimmt uns zusammen wie ein Bogenstrich,
der aus zwei Saiten eine Stimme zieht.
Auf welches Instrument sind wir gespannt?
Und welcher Geiger hat uns in der Hand?
O süßes Lied.

Before the Summer Rain

Suddenly from all greens of the park
a something, one does not know what, is missing;
one feels the park come closer to the windows
and keep its silence. Urgently and sharp,

the plover's voice resounds out of the trees,
putting into one's mind a St. Jerome:
so zeal and solitude together pour
from the one voice to which the storm concedes

a place. The walls of this wide chamber seem
with the hung pictures to have stepped away
as if to hear us talking were taboo.

The tapestries, gone pale now, yet display
the faint, uncertain light of afternoons
like those which, fearsome, in one's childhood gleamed.

Vor dem Sommerregen

Auf einmal ist aus allem Grün im Park
man weiß nicht was, ein Etwas, fortgenommen;
man fühlt ihn näher an die Fenster kommen
und schweigsam sein. Inständig nur und stark

ertönt aus dem Gehölz der Regenpfeifer,
man denkt an einen Hieronymus:
so sehr steigt irgend Einsamkeit und Eifer
aus dieser einen Stimme, die der Guß

erhören wird. Des Saales Wände sind
mit ihren Bildern von uns fortgetreten,
als dürften sie nicht hören was wir sagen.

Es spiegeln die verblichenen Tapeten
das ungewisse Licht von Nachmittagen,
in denen man sich fürchtete als Kind.

Death Experience

We know nothing of this departing, that
does not confide in us. We have no grounds
for showing admiration, love, or hate
to death, which is so wondrously deformed

by its masked mouth of high-tragic lament.
Yet is the world full of roles that we play.
As long as we care if we please, this day,
death too acts, though to please not its intent.

But when you left, there burst onto this stage
a strip of realism through the crack
you went through: green of realistic shade,
of realistic sun, of real woods' bark.

We go on acting, the fearsome, hard learned
reciting and stage gestures now and then
raising; but your existence, far-off turned
and not observing what we play, yet can

sometimes look at us here, a revelation
of that reality let down unsought
so that we in a brief illumination
act out our life, giving applause no thought.

Todes-Erfahrung

Wir wissen nichts von diesem Hingehn, das
nicht mit uns teilt. Wir haben keinen Grund,
Bewunderung und Liebe oder Haß
dem Tod zu zeigen, den ein Maskenmund

tragischer Klage wunderlich entstellt.
Noch ist die Welt voll Rollen, die wir spielen.
Solang wir sorgen, ob wir auch gefielen,
spielt auch der Tod, obwohl er nicht gefällt.

Doch als du gingst, da brach in diese Bühne
ein Streifen Wirklichkeit durch jenen Spalt
durch den du hingingst: Grün wirklicher Grüne,
wirklicher Sonnenschein, wirklicher Wald.

Wir spielen weiter. Bang und schwer Erlerntes
hersagend und Gebärden dann und wann
aufhebend; aber dein von uns entferntes,
aus unserm Stück entrücktes Dasein kann

uns manchmal überkommen, wie ein Wissen
von jener Wirklichkeit sich niedersenkend,
so daß wir eine Weile hingerissen
das Leben spielen, nicht an Beifall denkend.

Roman Sarcophagi

What, though, restrains us from believing that
(thus are we set down here, commanded thus)
not for a short time only stress and hate
and this confusedness abide in us,

as once in this sarcophagus, arrayed
with rings and ribbons, gods' heads, festive cups,
in garments slowly being eaten up
a slowly rotting object lay—

until the unknown mouths should swallow it,
who never speak. (Where does there be and think
a mind to put them one day into use?)

There, ancient aqueducts were made to emit
eternal water, turned into those ranks—:
that still reflects and shines in them, and moves.

Römische Sarkophage

Was aber hindert uns zu glauben, daß
(so wie wir hingestellt sind und verteilt)
nicht eine kleine Zeit nur Drang und Haß
und dies Verwirrende in uns verweilt,

wie einst in dem verzierten Sarkophag
bei Ringen, Götterbildern, Gläsern, Bändern,
in langsam sich verzehrenden Gewändern
ein langsam Aufgelöstes lag—

bis es die unbekannten Munde schluckten,
die niemals reden. (Wo besteht und denkt
ein Hirn, um ihrer einst sich zu bedienen?)

Da wurde von den alten Aquädukten
ewiges Wasser in sie eingelenkt—:
das spiegelt jetzt und geht und glänzt in ihnen.

Departure

How have I felt it, what departure means.
How do I yet: a dark never-undone
ferocious something, which a close-bound one
shows and shows and delays and rips to pieces.

How was I then defenseless, to see one
that even as she called me let me go,
stayed back, as if all womankind in one
and nonetheless was small, and white, and so:

A wave, not any longer meant for me,
a soft re-waving—, hardly by now, too,
explicable: perhaps a small plum tree
from which in haste a cuckoo just now flew.

Abschied

Wie hab ich das gefühlt was Abschied heißt.
Wie weiß ichs noch: ein dunkles unverwundnes
grausames Etwas, das ein Schönverbundnes
noch einmal zeigt und hinhält und zerreißt.

Wie war ich ohne Wehr, dem zuzuschauen,
das, da es mich, mich rufend, gehen ließ,
zurückblieb, so als wärens alle Frauen
und dennoch klein und weiß und nichts als dies:

Ein Winken, schon nicht mehr auf mich bezogen,
ein leise Weiterwinkendes—, schon kaum
erklärbar mehr: vielleicht ein Pflaumenbaum,
von dem ein Kuckuck hastig abgeflogen.

The Poet

You move away from me, oh Hour.
Your wing stroke strikes wounds into me.
But then: what should I make of my mouth?
what of my night? what of my day?

I have no loved one, have no house,
no place at all where I can stay.
All things to which I give away
myself get rich and hand me out.

Der Dichter

Du entfernst dich von mir, du Stunde.
Wunden schlägt mir dein Flügelschlag.
Allein: was soll ich mit meinem Munde?
mit meiner Nacht? mit meinem Tag?

Ich habe keine Geliebte, kein Haus,
keine Stelle auf der ich lebe.
Alle Dinge, an die ich mich gebe,
werden reich und geben mich aus.

The Donor

This work was ordered for the artists' guild.
Perhaps, then, Christ had not appeared to him;
perhaps no holy bishop to his side
came gently as in this scene is portrayed
and laid a reassuring hand on him.

The kneeling may be the whole thing: the skill
(so is it with all such things we once learned):
to kneel just so: so one's contours are turned,
those outward-yearning things, like horses spanned,
the traces held in heart as if in hand.

So if a horrible event takes place,
an unlooked-for one and till then unknown,
we yet can hope that it will not see us
but come yet nearer, come quite face to face,
sunk in itself, concerned with self alone.

Der Stifter

Das war der Auftrag an die Malergilde.
Vielleicht daß ihm der Heiland nie erschien;
vielleicht trat auch kein heiliger Bischof milde
an seine Seite wie in diesem Bilde
und legte leise seine Hand auf ihn.

Vielleicht war dieses alles: *so* zu knien
(so wie es alles ist was wir erfuhren):
zu knien: daß man die eigenen Konturen,
die auswärtswollenden, ganz angespannt
im Herzen hält, wie Pferde in der Hand.

Daß wenn ein Ungeheueres geschähe,
das nicht versprochen ist und nieverbrieft,
wir hoffen könnten, daß es uns nicht sähe
und näher käme, ganz in unsrer Nähe,
mit sich beschäftigt und in sich vertieft.

Saint Sebastian

Like a person lying down, he stands,
wholly proferred by that great resolve,
rapt as a mother with a nursing child,
and held together as a wreath in hand.

And the arrows come in: now and now
and as if they had sprung from his loins,
iron, aquiver in their open ends.
But he faintly smiles, unhurt somehow.

Only once, his pain becomes intense,
and his eyes are frankly suffering then,
till they put such things aside as petty
and as if disdainfully of them,
those destroyers of a thing of beauty.

Sankt Sebastian

Wie ein Liegender so steht er; ganz
hingehalten von dem großen Willen.
Weitenrückt wie Mütter, wenn sie stillen,
und in sich gebunden wie ein Kranz.

Und die Pfeile kommen: jetzt und jetzt
und als sprängen sie aus seinen Lenden,
eisern bebend mit den freien Enden.
Doch er lächelt dunkel, unverletzt.

Einmal nur wird seine Trauer groß,
und die Augen liegen schmerzlich bloß,
bis sie etwas leugnen, wie Geringes,
und als ließen sie verächtlich los
die Vernichter eines schönen Dinges.

Buddha

As if he heard. Silence: a thing far away…
We can no longer hear it as we pause.
And he is Star. And over him array
themselves huge stars, invisible to us.

Oh he is All. Truly now, should we wait
for him to see us? Would he feel the need?
And if we here fell face-down at his feet,
he would stay deep as if in some beast's state.

For that that to his feet has wrenched us thus
has run its course through him for countless years.
He, who forgets our suffering here
and undergoes what exiles us.

Buddha

Als ob er horchte. Stille: eine Ferne…
Wir halten ein und hören sie nicht mehr.
Und er ist Stern. Und andre große Sterne,
die wir nicht sehen, stehen um ihn her.

O er ist Alles. Wirklich, warten wir,
daß er uns sähe? Sollte er bedürfen?
Und wenn wir hier uns vor ihm niederwürfen,
er bliebe tief und träge wie ein Tier.

Denn das, was uns zu seinen Füßen reißt,
das kreist in ihm seit Millionen Jahren.
Er, der vergißt was wir erfahren
und der erfährt was uns verweist.

The Carousel

Luxembourg Gardens

Under a roof and in its shade revolves
for just a little period the band
of horses, colorful, all from the land
that lingers a long time ere it dissolves.
Many indeed are yoked to wagons, and
yet all have fortitude upon their faces;
a fierce red lion keeps up with their paces,
and now and then an all-white elephant.

A stag, even, is there, as in the fen,
except he bears a saddle, and on that
a small blue maiden, well and fast strapped in.

Upon the lion a boy rides, white and young,
bracing himself with his small, hot hand,
while under him the beast shows teeth and tongue.

And now and then an all-white elephant.

And on the horses they come riding past,
girls, too, all radiant, to the rearings cling
though grown almost too old; amid each swing
they look up, overhead, this way and that—

And now and then an all-white elephant.

And it goes on and rushes toward its end
and turns and circles, just that, with no goal.
Passing, a red, a green, a gray are sent,
a small profile, barely as yet formed whole.
And now and then a smile comes, this way bent,
a blessed one that dazzles, freely lent
within this breathless and unseeing spiel.

Das Karussell

Jardin du Luxembourg

Mit einem Dach und seinem Schatten dreht
sich eine kleine Weile der Bestand
von bunten Pferden, alle aus dem Land,
das lange zögert, eh es untergeht.
 Zwar manche sind an Wagen angespannt,
doch alle haben Mut in ihren Mienen;
ein böser roter Löwe geht mit ihnen
und dann und wann ein weißer Elefant.

Sogar ein Hirsch ist da, ganz wie im Wald,
nur daß er einen Sattel trägt und drüber
ein kleines blaues Mädchen aufgeschnallt.

Und auf dem Löwen reitet weiß ein Junge
und hält sich mit der kleinen heißen Hand,
dieweil der Löwe Zähne zeigt und Zunge.

Und dann und wann ein weißer Elefant.

Und auf den Pferden kommen sie vorüber,
auch Mädchen, helle, diesem Pferdesprunge
fast schon entwachsen; mitten in dem Schwunge
schauen sie auf, irgendwohin, herüber—

Und dann und wann ein weißer Elefant.

Und das geht hin und eilt sich, daß es endet,
und kreist und dreht sich nur und hat kein Ziel.
Ein Rot, ein Grün, ein Grau vorbeigesendet,
ein kleines kaum begonnenes Profil—,
Und manchesmal ein Lächeln, hergewendet,
ein seliges, das blendet und verschwendet
an dieses atemlose blinde Spiel.

FROM **New Poems, Second Part**
AUS **Neue Gedichte, Zweiter Teil**

Black Cat

A phantom, still, is only like a spot
on which your glance jolts to a clanging halt;
here, on the other hand, on this black coat
the firmest gaze you summon falls apart:

like a frenzied man when in the height
of rage he stamps his way into the black
and instantly the deep pads all about
the cell wall smother and dissolve the shock.

Our gazes that we turned her way, all those,
she seems somehow to take in and conceal
so that while vexed and sullen, menacing,
she turns her eyes on them and, doing so, drowses.
But suddenly as if aroused she turns
her face, bluntly encountering your own:
and there you meet your gaze within the pale
gold amber of her roundly jeweled one
surprisingly once more: shut tightly in
like some insect extinct these eons since.

Schwarze Katze

Ein Gespenst ist noch wie eine Stelle,
dran dein Blick mit einem Klange stößt;
aber da, an diesem schwarzen Felle
wird dein stärkstes Schauen aufgelöst:

wie ein Tobender, wenn er in vollster
Raserei ins Schwarze stampft,
jählings am benehmenden Gepolster
einer Zelle aufhört und verdampft.

Alle Blicke, die sie jemals trafen,
scheint sie also an sich zu verhehlen,
um darüber drohend und verdrossen
zuzuschauern und damit zu schlafen.
Doch auf einmal kehrt sie, wie geweckt,
ihr Gesicht und mitten in das deine:
und da triffst du deinen Blick im geelen
Amber ihrer runden Augensteine
unerwartet wieder: eingeschlossen
wie ein ausgestorbenes Insekt.

A Wrinkled Woman

Lightly, as if she has died
she bears the glove, the shawl.
From her bureau, an airy tide
has taken the place of all

the aroma she knew herself in.
She long since does not ask who
she is (: some distant kin),
and in deep thought walks through

and tends a demanding room,
which she orders and keeps,
since it may well have come
that here the same maiden sleeps.

Eine Welke

Leicht, wie nach ihrem Tode
trägt sie die Handschuh, das Tuch.
Ein Duft aus ihrer Kommode
verdrängte den lieben Geruch,

an dem sie sich früher erkannte.
Jetzt fragte sie lange nicht, wer
sie sei (: eine ferne Verwandte),
und geht in Gedanken umher

und sorgt für ein ängstliches Zimmer,
das sie ordnet und schont,
weil es vielleicht noch immer
dasselbe Mädchen bewohnt.

Archaic Torso of Apollo

We did not know his head, denied us here,
in which the two eye-apples ripened. But
his torso shines yet, like a chandelier
in which his gaze, though it is screwed tight-shut,

endures and gleams. If not, the breast's fine prow
could never blind you, and the silent twist
of loins could not have sent a smile on past
into the parts that were creation's how.

If not, this stone would stand maimed and untall
beneath the shoulders' undisguised downfall
and not glow back thus like a wild beast's fur;

and would not burst from all its rims, ablaze
as a bright star: for from no angle there
are you not seen. You must amend your ways.

Archäischer Torso Apollos

Wir kannten nicht sein unerhörtes Haupt,
darin die Augenäpfel reiften. Aber
sein Torso glüht noch wie ein Kandelaber,
in dem sein Schauen, nur zurückgeschraubt,

sich hält und glänzt. Sonst könnte nicht der Bug
der Brust dich blenden, und im leisen Drehen
der Lenden könnte nicht ein Lächeln gehen
zu jener Mitte, die die Zeugung trug.

Sonst stünde dieser Stein entstellt und kurz
unter der Schultern durchsichtigem Sturz
und flimmerte nicht so wie Raubtierfelle;

und bräche nicht aus allen seinen Rändern
aus wie ein Stern: denn da ist keine Stelle,
die dich nicht sieht. Du muß dein Leben ändern.

Corpse-Washing

They had grown used to him, but when the flame
of the lamp from the kitchen flickeringly burned
in the dark draft, the unknown person turned
unknown indeed. They washed his neck. His name

and lot being unknown to them, they tried
to guess what they thought probable enough,
ceaselessly washing. One needed to cough
and let the vinegary sponge a moment ride

upon his face. Then, momentarily,
the other paused, too. From her stiff brush burst
loud drops, and all the while his horribly
clenched, twisted hand seemed to will them to see,
all in that house, that he had no more thirst.

He proved it so. As if embarrassed, they
with a short cough bent to their duty faster
so on the wallpaper, as if in play,
their crooked shadows crossed the silent patterns

turning and wallowing as in a net,
until at last the washers' work was done.
In the uncurtained window frame, night hung
unfeelingly. And one, his name unknown,
lay bare and cleansed there and gave orders out.

Leichen-Wäsche

Sie hatten sich an ihn gewöhnt. Doch als
die Küchenlampe kam und unruhig brannte
im dunkeln Luftzug, war der Unbekannte
ganz unbekannt. Sie wuschen seinen Hals,

und da sie nichts von seinem Schicksal wußten,
so logen sie ein anderes zusamm,
fortwährend waschend. Eine mußte husten
und ließ solang den schweren Essigschwamm

auf dem Gesicht. Da gab es eine Pause
auch für die zweite. Aus der harten Bürste
klopften die Tropfen; während seine grause
gekrampfte Hand dem ganzen Hause
beweisen wollte, daß ihn nicht mehr dürste.

Und er bewies. Sie nahmen wie betreten
eiliger jetzt mit einem kurzen Huster
die Arbeit auf, so daß an den Tapeten
ihr krummer Schatten in dem stummen Muster

sich wand und wälzte wie in einem Netze,
bis daß die Waschenden zu Ende kamen.
Die Nacht im vorhanglosen Fensterrahmen
war rücksichtslos. Und einer ohne Namen
lag bar und reinlich da und gab Gesetze.

Piano Practice

Summer hums. The late day makes one tired;
she sniffed distractedly at her fresh dress
and put into each finely wrought etude
impatience for some thing of solidness

that might appear tomorrow, might this evening,
that might be present, though somehow concealed;
and out the window, tall and full of meaning,
the coddled park was suddenly revealed.

She broke off, closed her hands, and gazed out there,
wishing she had a lengthy book to read,
and, angry, shoved the jasmine scent aside.
It made her ill, she had become aware.

Übung am Klavier

Der Sommer summt. Der Nachmittag macht müde;
sie atmete verwirrt ihr frisches Kleid
und legte in die triftige Etüde
die Ungeduld nach einer Wirklichkeit,

die kommen konnte: morgen, heute abend—,
die vielleicht da war, die man nur verbarg;
und vor den Fenstern, hoch und alles habend,
empfand sie plötzlich den verwöhnten Park.

Da brach sie ab; schaute hinaus, verschränkte
die Hände; wünschte sich ein langes Buch—
und schob auf einmal den Jasmingeruch
erzürnt zurück. Sie fand, daß er sie kränkte.

Leda

As he prepared to enter her in his need,
he felt afraid almost, the swan was so fair;
deeply unsure, he vanished inside, there.
Now, though, his trickery tricked him to the deed,

when he as yet had not looked at this being's
unthought-of self. And she, the open one,
recognized who was nearing in the swan
and knew he was petitioning for something

that she, confusedly resisting him,
no longer could conceal. He settled now,
embraced her through her weakening defense

and in the one adored found his release.
Finally then he joyed in plume and down,
becoming truly swan in her embrace.

Leda

Als ihn der Gott in seiner Not betrat,
erschrak er fast, den Schwan so schön zu finden;
er ließ sich ganz verwirrt in ihm verschwinden.
Schon aber trug ihn sein Betrug zur Tat,

bevor er noch des unerprobten Seins
Gefühle prüfte. Und die Aufgetane
erkannte schon den Kommenden im Schwane
und wußte schon: er bat um Eins,

das sie, verwirrt in ihrem Widerstand,
nicht mehr verbergen konnte. Er kam nieder
und halsend durch die immer schwächre Hand

ließ sich der Gott in die Geliebte los.
Dann erst empfand er glücklich sein Gefieder
und wurde wirklich Schwan in ihrem Schooß.

The Burned-Over Place

Avoided by the early-autumn dawn,
which was in doubt, there lay behind black rows
of linden trees, close up to the farmhouse,
newness, a vacancy. Yet one more ground

on which the children, come God knows where from,
yelled at each other, over fragments wrestling.
But all turned quiet each time he would come,
the son of the place, from half-turned-to-ashes

rafters dragging off pots and bent-up kettles
by means of a long, fallen, forkéd bough,—
and looking, then, around as if deception
made him see those, whom his appearance now

caused to imagine what had once stood there.
It seemed to him, since it was there no more,
eerie: phantasm-like as a pharaoh.
And he was someone else. As fom afar.

Die Brandstätte

Gemieden von dem Frühherbstmorgen, der
mißtrauisch war, lag hinter den versengten
Hauslinden, die das Heidehaus beengten,
ein Neues, Leeres. Eine Stelle mehr,

auf welcher Kinder, von Gott weiß woher,
einander zuschrien und nach Fetzen haschten.
Doch alle wurden stille, sooft er,
der Sohn von hier, aus heißen, halbveraschten

Gebälken Kessel und verbogne Tröge
an einem langen Gabelaste zog,—
um dann mit einem Blick als ob er löge
die andern anzusehn, die er bewog

zu glauben, was an dieser Stelle stand.
Denn seit es nicht mehr war, schien es ihm so
seltsam: phantastischer als Pharao.
Und er war anders. Wie aus fernem Land.

Lady on a Balcony

Suddenly she steps forth, wrapped in air
and as if picked out, bright in the brightness,
while the chamber, as if from politeness,
fills the doorway back of her

darkly as a cameo's dark base,
at whose edge there seeps a shimmer through;
you say evening had not taken place
till she came to yield herself up to

what for her the parapet conferred,
hands there too,—as to seem free of all weight:
rows of houses having held her straight
heavenward, to be by all bestirred.

Dame auf einem Balkon

Plötzlich tritt sie, in den Wind gehüllt,
licht in Lichtes, wie herausgegriffen,
während jetzt die Stube wie geschliffen
hinter ihr die Türe füllt

dunkel wie der Grund einer Kamee,
die ein Schimmern durchläßt durch die Ränder;
und du meinst der Abend war nicht, ehe
sie heraustrat, um auf das Geländer

noch ein wenig von sich fortzulegen,
noch die Hände,—um ganz leicht zu sein:
wie dem Himmel von den Häuserreihn
hingereicht, von allem zu bewegen.

Lady before the Mirror

As one spices up a slumbrous drink
she turns softly loose into the fluid
clearness of the mirror her tired mood;
and therein she lets her best smile sink.

And she waits to see the flowingness
rise from there; and then pours out her hair
into the mirror and, her wondrous-fair
shoulder rising from her evening dress,

quietly drinks from her image—drinks
what a lover in all rapture might,
testing, with misgiving; and she thinks

to call her maid only when in the glass
lucidly her mirror shows the lights,
armoires, and sadness as the late hours pass.

Dame vor dem Spiegel

Wie in einem Schlaftrunk Spezerein
löst sie leise in dem flüssigklaren
Spiegel ihr ermüdetes Gebaren;
und sie tut ihr Lächeln ganz hinein.

Und sie wartet, daß die Flüssigkeit
davon steigt; dann gießt sie ihre Haare
in den Spiegel und, die wunderbare
Schulter hebend aus dem Abendkleid,

trinkt sie still aus ihrem Bild. Sie trinkt,
was ein Liebender im Taumel tränke,
prüfend, voller Mißtraun; und sie winkt

erst der Zofe, wenn sie auf dem Grunde
ihres Spiegels Lichter findet, Schränke
und das Trübe einer späten Stunde.

The Sundial

Seldom does a shower of damp mold
reach out of the garden's shady mass,
where drops hear drops fall, and songbirds pass,
singing, to the little pole
that in mint and coriander stands
showing summer's daily hours;

only when the lady (with a servant
close) bends low, the better to observe
patterns there amid the flowers,
darkness comes and hides the hours.

Or else when a summer-season rain
comes out of the undulating train
high up does it have a time to doze;
for it has no way to tell the hours
but when from the fruit- and blossom-bowers
in the garden house time comes and glows.

Die Sonnenuhr

Selten reicht ein Schauer feuchter Fäule
aus dem Gartenschatten, wo einander
Tropfen fallen hören und ein Wander-
vogel lautet, zu der Säule,
die in Majoran und Koriander
steht und Sommerstunden zeigt;

nur sobald die Dame (der ein Diener
nachfolgt) in dem hellen Florentiner
über ihren Rand sich neigt,
wird sie schattig und verschweigt—.

Oder wenn ein sommerlicher Regen
aufkommt aus dem wogenden Bewegen
hoher Kronen, hat sie eine Pause;
denn sie weiß die Zeit nicht auszudrücken,
die dann in den Frucht- und Blumenstücken
plötzlich glüht im weißen Gartenhause.

FROM **Uncollected Poems**
AUS **Nicht Eingesammelte Gedichte**

The Loved One's Death

He knew of death only what everyone knows:
that it takes us and thrusts us into silence.
But as she then, not wrenched away from him,
no, unloosed softly, gently from his eyes,

glided above to shades outside our ken,
and when he felt that over there they now
had her maidenly smile, so like a moon,
and her ways to do pleasure to,

to him then all the dead became as known
as if through her each of them had been made
close kin to him; he let the rest speak on

and paid no mind to them and called that land
the fortunately placed, forever sweet—
and with a touch tested it for her feet.

Der Tod der Geliebten

Er wußte nur vom Tod, was alle wissen:
daß er uns nimmt und in das Stumme stößt.
Als aber sie, nicht von ihm fortgerissen,
nein, leis aus seinen Augen ausgelöst,

hinüberglitt zu unbekannten Schatten,
und als er fühlte, daß sie drüben nun
wie einen Mond ihr Mädchenlächeln hatten
und ihre Weise wohlzutun:

da wurden ihm die Toten so bekannt,
als wäre er durch sie mit einem jeden
ganz nah verwandt; er ließ die andern reden

und glaubte nicht und nannte jenes Land
das gutgelegene, das immersüße—
Und tastete es ab für ihre Füße.

Untitled ["Death is great"]

Death is great.
We are in his keep
and we laugh.
When we think our lives are middle-deep,
he dares to weep
down in our selves.

Ohne Titel ["Der Tod ist groß"]

Der Tod ist groß.
Wir sind die Seinen
lachenden Munds.
Wenn wir uns mitten im Leben meinen,
wagt er zu weinen
mitten in uns.

Untitled ["Workmen we are"]

Workmen we are: novices, masters, doers,
constructing you, you high cathedral wall.
Sometimes there comes an earnest traveler to us,
to our massed spirits, moves like radiance through us,
and shows us trembling a new grasp for all.

We climb then up the gently rocking frame,
the hammer hanging heavy in our grip,
until a given hour shall kiss our brows
and shimmering as in all wisdom's name
arrive from you as wind to a ship.

Our many hammers sound then an echo
that passes through the mountains spate on spate.
Only at evening do we let you go:
and all your future contours start to glow.

God, thou art great.

Ohne Titel ["Werkleute sind wir"]

Werkleute sind wir: Knappen, Jünger, Meister,
und bauen dich, du hohes Mittelschiff.
Und manchmal kommt ein ernster Hergereister,
geht wie ein Glanz durch unsre hundert Geister
und zeigt uns zitternd einen neuen Griff.

Wir steigen in die wiegenden Gerüste,
in unsern Händen hängt der Hammer schwer,
bis eine Stunde uns die Stirnen küßte,
die strahlend und als ob sie alles wüßte
von dir kommt wie der Wind vom Meer.

Dann ist ein Hallen von den vielen Hämmern,
und durch die Berge geht es Stoß um Stoß
Erst wenn es dunkelt, lassen wir dich los:
und deine kommenden Konturen dämmern.

Gott, du bist groß.

Untitled
["That which the flying birds"]

That which the flying birds cast themselves through
is not the space that brings your self to flower.
(Yonder, outdoors, you own your self no more
and fade away, return denied to you.)

Space steps from us and translates things anew:
to make a tree's existence live by you,
throw inner space around it from that free
space that you shelter. Wrap it, thus, with order.
It sets itself no bounds. Only as bordered
with what you've yielded can it be true tree.

Ohne Titel
["Durch den sich Vögel werfen"]

Durch den sich Vögel werfen, ist nicht der
vertraute Raum, der die Gestalt dir steigert.
(Im Freien, dorten, bist du dir verweigert
und schwindest weiter ohne Wiederkehr.)

Raum greift aus uns und übersetzt die Dinge:
daß dir das Dasein eines Baums gelinge,
wirf Innenraum um ihn, aus jenem Raum,
der in dir west. Umgieb ihn mit Verhaltung.
Er grenzt sich nicht. Erst in der Eingestaltung
in dein Verzichten wird er wirklich Baum.

Untitled ["Tears, tears that burst"]

Tears, tears that burst out of me.
My death, Moor, transporting
my heart, hold me more sloping,
so they can flow down. I want to speak.

Black giant, heart in your hand.
Even if I will have spoken,
do you believe the silence was broken?

Rock me, old man.

Ohne Titel ["Tränen, Tränen die aus mir brechen"]

Tränen, Tränen die aus mir brechen.
Mein Tod, Mohr, Träger
meines Herzens, halte mich schräger,
daß sie abfließen. Ich will sprechen.

Schwarzer, riesiger Herzhalter.
Wenn ich auch spräche,
glaubst du denn, daß das Schweigen bräche?

Wiege mich, Alter.

Untitled ["Lifting my glance"]

Lifting my glance from the book, from the close-up, countable lines,
into the full-blown night out there:
How in the measure of stars are our urgent feelings' designs,
like untying the cords
that bound sprays wear:

Youth of the buoyant and bowing sway of the heavy
and the sweetly hesitant front—.
Everywhere striving for gain and not taking pleasure;
world too much and Earth enough.

Ohne Titel ["Hebend die Blicke"]

Hebend die Blicke vom Buch, von den nahen zählbaren Zeilen,
in die vollendete Nacht hinaus:
O wie sich sternegemäß die gedrängten Gefühle verteilen,
so als bände man auf
einen Bauernstrauß:

Jugend der leichten und neigendes Schwanken der schweren
und der zärtlichen zögernder Bug—.
Überall Lust zu Bezug und nirgends Begehren;
Welt zu viel und Erde genug.

Untitled ["We waken now"]

We waken now amid our memories
and turn our faces toward things that were;
whispering sweetness, by which we were seized
before, sits nearby, hushed, with unbound hair.

Ohne Titel ["Nun wachen wir"]

Nun wachen wir mit den Erinnerungen
und halten das Gesicht an das, was war;
flüsternde Süße, die uns einst durchdrungen,
sitzt schweigend neben mit gelöstem Haar.

Death

There stands death as a bluish extract in
a cup that does not have a proper base.
In, for a cup, a most unusual place:
upon the back of a hand. Well indeed, then,
you can yet see in that glazed swinging shape
the broken handle. Dusty. And: "With-hope,"
on its curved front in halfway rubbed-out script.

Those words the drinker, he whom that drink hit,
read off amid a distant breakfast once.

What are such beings, ones
you have to scare away with poison or spite?

If not, would they have stayed? In love, are they,
with a repast so full of clog, of hindrance?
You have to take the bitter present day
out of them like a set of ivory dentures.
They babble then. Guh-gheez, guh-gahrz.

....

O falling stars,
gazed at once from a bridge, all that array—:
Not to forget you. Stay!

Der Tod

Da steht der Tod, ein bläulicher Absud
in einer Tasse ohne Untersatz.
Ein wunderlicher Platz für eine Tasse:
steht auf dem Rücken einer Hand. Ganz gut
erkennt man noch an dem glasierten Schwung
den Bruch des Henkels. Staubig. Und: »Hoff-nung«
an ihrem Bug in aufgebrauchter Schrift.

Das hat der Trinker, den der Trank betrifft,
bei einem fernen Frühstück abgelesen.

Was sind denn das für Wesen,
die man zuletzt wegschrecken muß mit Gift?

Blieben sie sonst? Sind sie denn hier vernarrt
in dieses Essen voller Hindernis?
Man muß ihnen die harte Gegenwart
ausnehmen, wie ein künstliches Gebiß.
Dann lallen sie. Gelall, gelall...

....

O Sternenfall,
von einer Brücke einmal eingesehn—:
Dich nicht vergessen. Stehn!

Untitled
["Brother Body is poor"]

Brother Body is poor...: that means, be rich for him.
He was often the rich one: pardon him then
the poverty of his evil moments.
If he acts then as if he hardly knows us,
we can gently remind him of our in-commons.

Of course we are not one, but are two lone ones:
our consciousness and He;
how much, nonetheless, to each other do we
find owing,
as friends always do! And illness keeps on showing:
friends are hard things to be!

Ohne Titel
["Bruder Körper ist arm"]

Bruder Körper ist arm...: da heißt es, reich sein für ihn.
Oft war er der Reiche: so sei ihm verziehn
das Armsein seiner argen Momente.
Wenn er dann tut, als ob er uns kaum noch kennte,
darf man ihn leise erinnern an alles Gemeinsame.

Freilich wir sind nicht Eines, sondern zwei Einsame:
unser Bewußtsein und Er;
aber wie vieles, das wir einander weither
verdanken,
wie Freunde es tun! Und man erfährt im Erkranken:
Freunde haben es schwer!

Untitled
["The bird calls are beginning"]

The bird calls are beginning to sound thanks.
And are just right. We listen a long time.
(We with our costumes on and, oh! our masks!)
What are they calling? self-regarding whims

in part, sadness, much strength to our unspoken
hope that the half-closed future may yet glow.
And, at each pause, our hearing deems it so,
the hush is healed, that they have broken.

Ohne Titel
["Die Vogelrufe fangen an"]

Die Vogelrufe fangen an zu rühmen.
Und sind im Recht. Wir hören lange hin.
(Wir hinter Masken, ach, und in Kostümen!)
Was rufen sie? ein wenig Eigensinn,

ein wenig Wehmut und sehr viel Versprechen,
das an der halbverschlossnen Zukunft feilt.
Und zwischendurch in unserm Horchen heilt
das schöne Schweigen, das sie brechen.

Full Power

Ah, take away from us strikers of hours and counters.
Out there, of a morning, fervent youth in the hunters;
        amid the dogs' yelping come shouts.
If in the shouldered brush we could be coolly sprayed
and in the new and the open—in breezes of early day
        feel time for us clearly marked out!

Such things pertained then to us, easily gladdened so.
Not, in a small, rigid room, after a night full of no,
        a day of denying.
These things are always right, pressing on one close to life;
since they are living indeed, the ever-affirmed quarry strides
        into the stroke of its dying.

Vollmacht

Ach entzögen wir uns Zählern und Stundenschlägern.
Einen Morgen hinaus, heißes Jungsein mit Jägern,
        Rufen im Hundegekläff.
Daß im durchdrängten Gebüsch Kühle uns fröhlich besprühe,
und wir im Neuen und Frein—in den Lüften der Frühe
        fühlten den graden Betreff!

Solches war uns bestimmt. Leichte beschwingte Erscheinung.
Nicht, im starren Gelaß, nach einer Nacht voll Verneinung,
        ein verneinender Tag.
Diese sind ewig im Recht: dringend dem Leben Genahte;
weil sie Lebendige sind, tritt das unendlich bejahte
        Tier in den tödlichen Schlag.

Untitled
["Ah, loose in the wind"]

Ah, loose in the wind,
how much vain returning has been.
Things that repel us from here
stand with arms spread,
when we have gone away,
uncomprehendingly.
Because there is no path
back. All things carry us off,
and, left open late, the house
stays empty.

Ohne Titel
["Ach, im Wind gelöst"]

Ach, im Wind gelöst,
 wieviel vergebliche Wiederkehr.
Manches, was uns verstößt,
tut hinterher,
wenn wir vorüber sind,
ratlos did Arme auf.
Denn es giebt keinen Lauf
zurück. Alles hebt uns hinaus,
und das spät offene Haus
bleibt leer.

Wild Rosebush

How it stands there before the darkening
of the rainy evening, young and pure;
sending its tendrils forth with a generous swing
and yet in rosehood deep-sunk and secure;

the shallow blossoms, here an open one,
uncared-for, all of them, and never willed:
thus, by itself unendingly outdone,
and with its self-born restlessness unstilled,

it calls the wanderer, who in late-day
reflectiveness along the road comes past:
Oh, see me stand, how, safe and unafraid,
unguarded, all I need I've self-amassed.

Wilder Rosenbusch

Wie steht er da vor den Verdunkelungen
des Regenabends, jung und rein;
in seinen Ranken schenkend ausgeschwungen
und doch versunken in sein Rose-sein;

die flachen Blüten, da und dort schon offen,
jegliche ungewollt und ungepflegt:
so, von sich selbst unendlich übertroffen
und unbeschreiblich aus sich selbst erregt,

ruft er dem Wandrer, der in abendlicher
Nachdenklichkeit den Weg vorüberkommt:
Oh sieh mich stehn, sieh her, was bin ich sicher
und unbeschützt und habe was mir frommt.

Moonlit Night

Path in the garden, deep as a generous draught,
silently in the soft boughs an elusive touch.
Oh and the moon, the moon, the benches are half
blooming beneath its uncertain approach.

Silence, compelling. Up there, are you awake yet?
Starry and moved is the window in front of you.
Wind's hands contrive to move
onto your close-by face the distantest night.

Mondnacht

Weg in den Garten, tief wie ein langes Getränke,
leise im weichen Gezweig ein entgehender Schwung.
Oh und der Mond, der Mond, fast blühen die Bänke
von seiner zögernden Näherung.

Stille, wie drängt sie. Bist du jetzt oben erwacht?
Sternig und fühlend steht dir das Fenster entgegen.
Hände der Winde verlegen
an dein nahes Gesicht die entlegenste Nacht.

The King of Munster

The king's hair had been cut;
too loose now sat his crown
and bent his ears a bit,
ears in which now and then

the great, malicious racket
of hungry maws was heard.
For the sake of warmth he sat there
his right hand underneath,

sullen and wretchedly bottomed.
He no more felt himself real:
the lord in him was modest
and his coition was dull.

Der König von Münster

Der König war geschoren;
nun ging ihm die Krone zu weit
und bog ein wenig die Ohren,
in die von Zeit zu Zeit

gehässiges Gelärme
aus Hungermäulern fand.
Er saß, von wegen der Wärme,
auf seiner rechten Hand,

mürrisch und schwergesäßig.
Er fühlte sich nicht mehr echt:
der Herr in ihm war mäßig,
und der Beischlaf war schlecht.

Untitled
["That is yearning"]

That is yearning: to dwell in the surges
and have no mother country amid time.
And that is wishing: dialogue that merges
hours daily with the eternal and sublime.

And that is life. Till from a yesterday
the loneliest of all hours comes to be,
which, smiling other than its sisters' way,
looks silent toward eternity.

Ohne Titel
["Das ist die Sehnsucht"]

Das ist die Sehnsucht: wohnen im Gewoge
und keine Heimat haben in der Zeit.
Und das sind Wünsche: leise Dialoge
täglicher Stunden mit der Ewigkeit.

Und das ist Leben. Bis aus einem Gestern
die einsamste von allen Stunden steigt,
die, anders lächelnd als die andern Schwestern,
dem Ewigen entgegenschweigt.

Untitled
["You come and go"]

You come and go. The doors slip-to
in silence when you come to call.
You, among all those who walk through
hushed houses, are most hushed of all.

One can grow used to you, so much
as not to glance up from one's book,
whose images gain a blue touch
of beauty in your shadowed look;
for things bring out your tone with such
as now is loud and now is hushed.

Often, when my thoughts see you here,
your all-united form unfolds;
you move like pure and bright roe deer,
and I am darkened and am woods.

You are a wheel that I stand near:
among your many somber axles
one keeps on adding to its weight
and turning near my silent state,
and my most willing works keep waxing
as you appear and reappear.

Ohne Titel
["Du kommst und gehst"]

Du kommst und gehst. Die Türen fallen
viel sanfter zu, fast ohne Wehn.
Du bist der Leiseste von allen,
die durch die leisen Häuser gehn.

Man kann sich so an dich gewöhnen,
daß man nicht aus dem Buche schaut,
wenn seine Bilder sich verschönen,
von deinem Schatten überblaut;
weil dich die Dinge immer tönen
nur einmal leis und einmal laut.

Oft, wenn ich dich in Sinnen sehe,
verteilt sich deine Allgestalt;
Du gehst wie lauter lichte Rehe,
und ich bin dunkel und bin Wald.

Du bist ein Rad, an dem ich stehe:
von deinen vielen dunklen Achsen
wird immer wieder eine schwer
und dreht sich näher zu mir her,
und meine willigen Werke wachsen
von Wiederkehr zu Wiederkehr.

Knight

Rides forth the knight in dark-black steel
out into the clamorous world.
And there there are all things: the day and the dale
and the friend and the foe and the hall-laid meal
and the May and the maid and the wood and the Grail,
and God in his thousands of selves in all
the roads and streets is installed.

But in the armor the knight wears, deep under,
back of the darkest of rings,
crouches death and must ponder and ponder:
When will the sword blade swing
over the iron hedge,
the blade, strange, unfettering thing
that calls me from here in this nest
where through each hunched-over day,
through so many days, I must cling,—
so I at last may stretch
and play
and sing.

Ritter

Reitet der Ritter in schwarzem Stahl
hinaus in die rauschende Welt.
Und draußen ist alles: der Tag und das Tal
und der Freund und der Feind und das Mahl im Saal
und der Mai und die Maid und der Wald und der Gral,
und Gott ist selber vieltausendmal
an allen Straßen gestellt.

Doch in dem Panzer des Ritters drinnen,
hinter den finstersten Ringen,
hockt der Tod und muß sinnen und sinnen:
Wann wird die Klinge springen
über die Eisenhecke,
die fremde befreiende Klinge,
die mich aus meinem Verstecke
holt, drin ich so viele
gebückte Tage verbringe,—
daß ich mich endlich strecke
und spiele
und singe.

End of Autumn

For some time I have seen
change coming on all sides.
A something stands and abides
and kills and causes grief.

Now more and more are all
the gardens less themselves;
from the yellowings to the yellows'
gradual downfall:
how long the way for me.

Into the emptiness
I gaze along each way.
Almost to the distant seas
I see the earnest grave
debarring forbidding sky.

Ende des Herbstes

Ich sehe seit einer Zeit,
wie alles sich verwandelt.
Etwas steht auf und handelt
und tötet und tut Leid.

Von Mal zu Mal sind all
die Gärten nicht dieselben;
von den gilbenden zu der gelben
langsamen Verfall:
wie war der Weg mir weit.

Jetzt bin ich bei den leeren
und schaue durch alle Alleen.
Fast bis zu den fernen Meeren
kann ich den ernsten schweren
verwehrenden Himmel sehn.

The Deranged Ones

And they say nothing, because the partitions
each one have been extracted from their sense
and hours when their words might find comprehension
have begun and then gone hence.

Often at night they step to the window to see:
suddenly good is all about.
Their hands rest in reality
and their heart is high and set to pray
and their eyes are calm and looking out

on the unhoped-for, badly kept
garden in the calmed and peaceful square,
which, in reflection of the alien worlds,
is thriving once more and unfading there.

Die Irren

Und sie schweigen, weil die Scheidewände
weggenommen sind aus ihrem Sinn,
und die Stunden, da man sie verstände,
heben an und gehen hin.

Nächtens oft, wenn sie ans Fenster treten:
plötzlich ist es alles gut.
Ihre Hände liegen im Konkreten,
und das Herz ist hoch und könnte beten,
und die Augen schauen ausgeruht

auf den unverhofften, oftentstellten
Garten im beruhigten Geviert,
der im Widerschein der fremden Welten
weiterwächst und niemals sich verliert.

Madness

She always is thinking: I am...I am...
Who are you then, Marie?
    A queen! A queen!
    On your knees before me, on your knees!

She always is weeping: I was...I was...
Who were you then, Marie?
    A no-one's child, poor and bare I was,
    and I can't say how that could be.

And from such a child did there grow up, then,
a princess, to whom one kneels?
    Because all things are different
    when seen as a beggar sees.

Then things have given greatness to you,
and still you cannot say when?
    On a night, on a night, a whole night through,
    and they spoke otherwise to me then.
    I stepped out into the alley, and see:
    it's strung like a violin;
    then melody, melody was Marie...
    and danced across and again.
    The people were frightened and crept away,
    and clung to their houses like plants,—
    for only a queen is allowed that way
    to dance in the alleys: to dance!...

Der Wahnsinn

Sie muß immer sinnen: Ich bin...ich bin...
Wer bist du denn, Marie?
    Eine Königin, eine Königin!
    In die Kniee vor mir, in die Knie!

Sie muß immer weinen: Ich war...ich war...
Wer warst du denn, Marie?
    Ein Niemandskind, ganz arm und bar,
    und ich kann dir nicht sagen wie.

Und wurdest aus einem solchen Kind
eine Fürstin, vor der man kniet?
    Weil die Dinge alle anders sind,
    als man sie beim Betteln sieht.

So haben die Dinge dich groß gemacht,
und kannst du noch sagen wann?
    Eine Nacht, eine Nacht, über eine Nacht,—
    und sie sprachen mich anders an.
    Ich trat in die Gasse hinaus und sieh:
    die ist wie mit Saiten bespannt;
    da wurde Marie Melodie, Melodie...
    und tanzte von Rand zu Rand.
    Die Leute schlichen so ängstlich hin,
    wie hart an die Häuser gepflanzt,—
    denn das darf doch nur eine Königin,
    daß sie tanzt in den Gassen: tanzt!...

Sacrifice

Oh, how my body blossoms from each vein
more fragrantly since I have come to know you;
see what a slim, straight walk I now maintain,
and you, you only wait—: and then, who are you?

See, I feel how much I have departed,
how leaf by leaf I have lost all old things.
Only your smile stands there as pure as stars
over you and soon, too, over me.

Everything that through my childhood days
nameless still and like clear water gleams,
I call before the altar by your name,
the altar that your hair has touched with flame
and that your breasts have delicately wreathed.

Opfer

O wie blüht mein Leib aus jeder Ader
duftender, seitdem ich dich erkenn;
sieh, ich gehe schlanker und gerader,
und du wartest nur—: wer bist du, denn?

Sieh: ich fühle, wie ich mich entferne,
wie ich Altes, Blatt um Blatt, verlier.
Nur dein Lächeln steht wie lauter Sterne
über dir und bald auch über mir.

Alles was durch meine Kinderjahre
namenlos noch und wie Wasser glänzt,
will ich nach dir nennen am Altare,
der entzündet ist von deinem Haare
und mit deinen Brüsten leicht bekränzt.

FROM **The Sonnets to Orpheus**
AUS **Die Sonette an Orpheus**

I, 1

There a tree rose. Oh pure change and abiding!
Oh Orpheus sings! Oh tall tree in the ear!
And all was silent and yet in their hiding
new signs, new starts and alterings appeared.

Creatures of stillness pressed on from the clear,
transformed wood out of lair and hidden nest;
and there it followed that not by behest
of cunning were they hushed, nor yet of fear,

but that of hearing. Bellows, cries, and roarings
seemed small things in their hearts. And though just there
hardly a hut had been, to take this in,

a refuge of the darkest longing then
with entryway of which the sideposts shook—
for them you made great temples in their hearing.

I, 1

Da stieg ein Baum. O reine Übersteigung!
O Orpheus singt! O hoher Baum im Ohr!
Und alles schwieg. Doch selbst in der Verschweigung
ging neuer Anfang, Wink und Wandlung vor.

Tiere aus Stille drangen aus dem klaren
gelösten Wald von Lager und Genist;
und da ergab sich, daß sie nicht aus List
und nicht aus Angst in sich so leise waren,

sondern aus Hören. Brüllen, Schrei, Geröhr
schien klein in ihren Herzen. Und wo eben
kaum eine Hütte war, dies zu empfangen,

ein Unterschlupf aus dunkelstem Verlangen
mit einem Zugang, dessen Pfosten beben,—
da schufst du ihnen Tempel im Gehör.

I, 7

Praise, that's the thing! One well marked out for praise,
he went forth like the ore that comes from rocks'
silence. His heart, a press whose few days
bring wine to mankind in unending stocks.

Never his voice grows muted in the dust
when in the grip of godly inspiration.
All becomes vineyard, all becomes grape-must,
prime in his feeling South's warm maturation.

Not even in the tombs of kings' decay
is he found wrong for praising, nor yet may
shame strike when from the gods a shadow falls.

He is one of the yet surviving heralds,
who far beyond the doorways of the dead
bears dishes of praiseworthy fruits for all.

I, 7

Rühmen, das ists! Ein zum Rühmen Bestellter,
ging er hervor wie das Erz aus des Steins
Schweigen. Sein Herz, o vergängliche Kelter
eines den Menschen unendlichen Weins.

Nie versagt ihm die Stimme am Staube,
wenn ihn das göttliche Beispiel ergreift.
Alles wird Weinberg, alles wird Traube,
in seinem fühlenden Süden gereift.

Nicht in den Grüften der Könige Moder
straft ihm die Rühmung Lügen, oder
daß von den Göttern ein Schatten fällt.

Er ist einer der bleibenden Boten,
der noch weit in die Türen der Toten
Schalen mit rühmlichen Früchten hält.

I, 9

Only the one who has raised
the lyre among shades
may give back perfect praise
that never fades.

Only the one who has dined
on poppy with the dead
cannot now fail to find
faint chords once played.

Though what reflects from the pond
may blur before us:
know the reflection.

Only in double-land
have human voices
eternal protection.

I, 9

Nur wer die Leier schon hob
auch unter Schatten,
darf das unendliche Lob
ahnend erstatten.

Nur wer mit Toten vom Mohn
aß, von dem ihren,
wird nicht den leisesten Ton
wieder verlieren.

Mag auch die Spieglung im Teich
oft uns verschwimmen:
wisse das Bild.

Erst in dem Doppelbereich
werden die Stimmen
ewig und mild.

I, 14

With blossom, vine-leaf, fruit we go our way.
They speak not just the language of the year.
From gloom a thing of many hues appears
and has perhaps the flush of jealousy

upon it, of the dead, who prop the earth.
How could we know what part they have in it?
For much, much time now they have all seen fit
with set-free marrow to imbue the turf.

The question though is: do they like it thus?...
Does this work done by gloomy slaves, this fruit,
press forth clenched firmly to their lords, to us?

Are *they* the lords, who sleep among the roots
and from their vast store freely give to us
this hybrid thing of silent power and kisses?

I, 14

Wir gehen um mit Blume, Weinblatt, Frucht.
Sie sprechen nicht die Sprache nur des Jahres.
Aus Dunkel steigt ein buntes Offenbares
und hat vielleicht den Glanz der Eifersucht

der Toten an sich, die die Erde stärken.
Was wissen wir von ihrem Teil an dem?
Es ist seit lange ihre Art, den Lehm
mit ihrem freien Marke zu durchmärken.

Nun fragt sich nur: tun sie es gern?...
Drängt diese Frucht, ein Werk von schweren Sklaven,
geballt zu uns empor, zu ihren Herrn?

Sind *sie* die Herrn, die bei den Wurzeln schlafen,
und gönnen uns aus ihren Überflüssen
dies Zwischending aus stummer Kraft und Küssen?

I, 15

Wait... that tastes good... but now it's in flight.
Small music, please, only stamping and hum—:
Lasses, you warm ones, lasses, all gone dumb,
dance how the taste of this wise fruit is right.

Dance, then, the orange. Remember all, do,
how it, while half-drowned in self, has resisted,
itself, its own sweethood. You have possessed it.
It has deliciously merged into you.

Dance, then, the orange. The sunnier region,
throw it out of yourself, so the ripeness may shine
in air of its homeland. Unveiled, aglow,

fragrance on fragrance! Form a close kinship
with the innocent, unwilling rind,
with the juice filling the blest one so.

I, 15

Wartet..., das schmeckt... Schon ists auf der Flucht.
...Wenig Musik nur, ein Stampfen, ein Summen—:
Mädchen, ihr warmen, Mädchen, ihr stummen,
tanzt den Geschmack der erfahrenen Frucht!

Tanzt die Orange. Wer kann sie vergessen,
wie sie, ertrinkend in sich, sich wehrt
wider ihr Süßsein. Ihr habt sie besessen.
Sie hat sich köstlich zu euch bekehrt.

Tanzt die Orange. Die wärmere Landschaft,
werft sie aus euch, daß die reife erstrahle
in Lüften der Heimat! Erglühte, enthüllt

Düfte um Düfte! Schafft die Verwandtschaft
mit der reinen, sich weigernden Schale,
mit dem Saft, der die Glückliche füllt.

I, 18

Sir, do you hear the New's
loud agitation?
Heralds are coming to
lift high its station.

Hearing cannot stay clear
in this loud raging,
but every cog and gear
asks for our praising.

And the machine, observe,
rolls to avenge itself
stealing our shapes and health.

Though its strength comes from us,
let it, all passionless,
run on and serve.

I, 18

Hörst du das Neue, Herr,
dröhnen und beben?
Kommen Verkündiger,
die es erheben.

Zwar ist kein Hören heil
in dem Durchtobtsein,
doch der Maschinenteil
will jetzt gelobt sein.

Sieh, die Maschine:
wie sie sich wälzt und rächt
und uns entstellt und schwächt.

Hat sie aus uns auch Kraft,
sie, ohne Leidenschaft,
treibe und diene.

I, 19

Let the world recklessly change
like cloud figurations,
all that is finished descends
home to the Ancient.

Over the changes and stirs,
farther and freer,
your prelude always endures,
god with the lyre.

Grief, we do not understand,
nor is love clear to our heart;
what in death holds us apart

is never shown us.
Song only, over the land,
charms and is holy.

I, 19

Wandelt sich rasch auch die Welt
wie Wolkengestalten,
alles Vollendete fällt
heim zum Uralten.

Über dem Wandel und Gang,
weiter und freier,
währt noch dein Vor-Gesang,
Gott mit der Leier.

Nicht sind die Leiden erkannt,
nicht ist die Liebe gelernt,
und was im Tod uns entfernt,

ist nicht entschleiert.
Einzig das Lied überm Land
heiligt und feiert.

I, 21

Springtime has come again. The earth
is a child with poems memorized;
many, oh many...and for her work,
the long, hard learning, wins the prize.

How strict her teacher! White streaks grew
in his beard, we were glad of those.
Now, how to name the green, the blue,
we ask the questions: she knows, she knows!

Earth, with time free, fortunate one,
play with the children now. We want
to catch you, happy earth. Joy brings

success. Great teaching the teacher has done,
and what is printed in each plant,
in each tough stem, she sings it, sings!

I, 21

Frühling ist wiedergekommen. Die Erde
ist wie ein Kind, das Gedichte weiß;
viele, o viele... Für die Beschwerde
langen Lernens bekommt sie den Preis.

Streng war ihr Lehrer. Wir mochten das Weiße
an dem Barte des alten Manns.
Nun, wie das Grüne, das Blaue heiße,
dürfen wir fragen: sie kanns, sie kanns!

Erde, die frei hat, du glückliche, spiele
nun mit den Kindern. Wir wollen dich fangen,
fröhliche Erde. Dem Frohsten gelingts.

O, was der Lehrer sie lehrte, das Viele,
und was gedruckt steht in Wurzeln und langen
schwierigen Stämmen: sie singts, sie singts!

I, 24

Shall we reject our ancient friendship, the great
never beckoning gods, because they are unknown
to this tough steel, which we most strongly reared,
or own a sudden hope that a map will show them?

These, the most powerful friends, taking the dead
from us, never interfere with our ways.
All of our banquets, our baths, we have tossed them away,
and their envoys to us, for ages too slow, our treads

over and over outpace them. Lonelier then, on each other
fully dependent, and yet we all are strangers,
we do not wander down paths anymore as lovely

ambles but straight ways. And only in boilers linger
the fires of before and brandish the burgeoning hammers.
We, though, are always declining in power, like swimmers.

I, 24

Sollen wir unsere uralte Freundschaft, die großen
niemals werbenden Götter, weil sie der harte
Stahl, den wir streng erzogen, nicht kennt, verstoßen
oder sie plötzlich suchen auf einer Karte?

Diese gewaltigen Freunde, die uns die Toten
nehmen, rühren nirgends an unsere Räder.
Unsere Gastmähler haben wir weit—, unsere Bäder,
fortgerückt, und ihre uns lang schon zu langsamen Boten

überholen wir immer. Einsamer nun auf einander
ganz angewiesen, ohne einander zu kennen,
führen wir nicht mehr die Pfade als schöne Mäander,

sondern als Grade. Nur noch in Dampfkesseln brennen
die einstigen Feuer und heben die Hämmer, die immer
größern. Wir aber nehmen an Kraft ab, wie Schwimmer.

I, 25

I shall again remember *you*, whom I knew
as I know a flower whose name I cannot recall,
and I wish *once* more to show them, stolen one, you,
lovely playmate of the unconquerable yell.

At first a dancer, who sharply, all doubtings and wavers,
left off, as if her youngness were cast in bronze;
mourning and listening—. Then from the lofty Enablers,
music of hers fell into her new-altered heart.

Illness was near. Now taken over by shadow,
darkened, her blood pressed on, but, as briefly suspicious,
drove forth again into springtime, its natural state.

Over and over, with crashes and dark interrupting,
earthly it glimmered. Till, after much frightful thumping,
it went through the open, uncaring gate.

I, 25

Dich aber will ich nun, *Dich*, die ich kannte
wie eine Blume, von der ich den Namen nicht weiß,
noch *ein* Mal erinnern und ihnen zeigen, Entwandte,
schöne Gespielin des unüberwindlichen Schrei's.

Tänzerin erst, die plötzlich, den Körper voll Zögern,
anhielt, als göß man ihr Jungsein in Erz;
trauernd und lauschend—. Da, von den hohen Vermögern
fiel ihr Musik in das veränderte Herz.

Nah war die Krankheit. Schon von den Schatten bemächtigt,
drängte verdunkelt das Blut, doch, wie flüchtig verdächtigt,
trieb es in seinen natürlichen Frühling hervor.

Wieder und wieder, von Dunkel und Sturz unterbrochen,
glänzte es irdisch. Bis es nach schrecklichem Pochen
trat in das trostlos offene Tor.

II, 2

Just as at times from the Master the pressing
forthcoming page takes away the *real*
stroke: often mirrors take the holy,
once-only smile of the girls away,

when they sample the morning, alone,—
or in the glow of the helpful lights.
And to the breathing of actual faces,
later, merely an afterglow falls.

What have eyes seen once in the limned
gradual fading of the corner fires:
glimpses of life, forever lost.

Ah, of the earth, who knows the losses?
Only he who yet would in praise
sing a heart that was born into the all.

II, 2

So wie dem Meister manchmal das eilig
nähere Blatt den *wirklichen* Strich
abnimmt: so nehmen oft Spiegel das heilig
einzige Lächeln der Mädchen in sich,

wenn sie den Morgen erproben, allein,—
oder im Glanze der dienenden Lichter.
Und in das Atmen der echten Gesichter,
später, fällt nur ein Widerschein.

Was haben Augen einst ins umrußte
lange Verglühn der Kamine geschaut:
Blicke des Lebens, für immer verlorne.

Ach, der Erde, wer kennt die Verluste?
Nur, wer mit dennoch preisendem Laut
sänge das Herz, das ins Ganze geborne.

II, 4

This is the animal that does not be.
They did not know it, but loved nonetheless
its neck, its bearing, its changeableness,
the quiet stillness of its scrutiny.

Indeed it *did* not be. But their regard
let it become all beast. They gave it slack.
And with that slack, clearly and freely spared,
it lightly raised its head, with little lack

of realness. They sustained it, not with corn,
just with the open chance that it might be.
And that chance gave such powers to the beast,

its brow produced a horn. A unique horn.
It whitely came before a virgin's eye—
and in her mirror was, and in her breast.

II, 4

O dieses ist das Tier, das es nicht giebt.
Sie wußtens nicht und habens jeden Falls
—sein Wandeln, seine Haltung, seinen Hals,
bis in des stillen Blickes Licht—geliebt.

Zwar *war* es nicht. Doch weil sie's liebten, ward
ein reines Tier. Sie ließen immer Raum.
Und in dem Raume, klar und ausgespart,
erhob es leicht sein Haupt und brauchte kaum

zu sein. Sie nährten es mit keinem Korn,
nur immer mit der Möglichkeit, es sei.
Und die gab solche Stärke an das Tier,

daß es aus sich ein Stirnhorn trieb. Ein Horn.
Zu einer Jungfrau kam es weiß herbei—
und war im Silber-Spiegel und in ihr.

II, 6

Rose, o sovereign, to people in old days
you were a cup with a plain, simple rim.
To *us*, though, you are the full and countless rays,
a never-to-be exhausted theme.

In all your richness you seem like clothes upon clothes
around a body that brightens the air;
yet every petal of yours at the same time shows
the shunning and denial of all such wear.

For centuries your fragrance has sent out
its sweetest names to all us here;
suddenly it floats like fame all about.

And yet we do not know its name, though we scour...
And recall makes it disappear,
what we implored of the callable hours.

II, 6

Rose, du thronende, denen im Altertume
warst du ein Kelch mit einfachem Rand.
Uns aber bist du die volle zahllose Blume,
der unerschöpfliche Gegenstand.

In deinem Reichtum scheinst du wie Kleidung um Kleidung
um einen Leib aus nichts als Glanz;
aber dein einzelnes Blatt ist zugleich die Vermeidung
und die Verleugnung jedes Gewands.

Seit Jahrhunderten ruft uns dein Duft
seine süßesten Namen herüber;
plötzlich liegt er wie Ruhm in der Luft.

Dennoch, wir wissen ihn nicht zu nennen, wir raten...
Und Erinnerung geht zu ihm über,
die wir von rufbaren Stunden erbaten.

II, 20

Distance between stars, how far; and yet how many times farther,
what we experience here.
One, for example, one child...and thereafter another,
off, oh, unthinkably far.

Fate, it may measure us by our existing's short span,
so fate seems strange to us;
think only how many spans between maiden and man,
whom she avoids and loves.

All is afar—, and nowhere the circle comes shut.
See in the bowl, on the table arrayed in gay dishes,
the fish's face's mystique.

Fish are all mute...who knows, but so we once thought.
But at the end is there not a place where we that that the fishes'
speech would have been, *without* it, speak?

II, 20

Zwischen den Sternen, wie weit; und doch, um wievieles noch weiter,
was man am Hiesigen lernt.
Einer, zum Beispiel, ein Kind...und ein Nächster, ein Zweiter—,
o wie unfaßlich entfernt.

Schicksal, es mißt uns vielleicht mit des Seienden Spanne,
daß es uns fremd erscheint;
denk, wieviel Spannen allein vom Mädchen zum Manne,
wenn es ihn meidet und meint.

Alles ist weit—, und nirgends schließt sich der Kreis.
Sieh in der Schüssel, auf heiter bereitetem Tische,
seltsam der Fische Gesicht.

Fische sind stumm..., meinte man einmal. Wer weiß?
Aber ist nicht am Ende ein Ort, wo man das, was der Fische
Sprache wäre, *ohne* sie spricht?

II, 23

Summon me to that one of your hours
that opposes you without a stay;
coming close with doglike, pleading airs
but always thereafter pulled away

when you think it's almost in your hand.
Thus things withheld from us are mostly yours.
We are free. We were sent from that land
where we once thought welcome would be ours.

Frightened, we request from you a hold,
we, too young sometimes for things of old,
and too old for what has never been.

We, made just with what we prize alone,
ah, for we are bough, are steel well-honed,
and are danger, ripening, sweet thing.

II, 23

Rufe mich zu jener deiner Stunden,
die dir unaufhörlich widersteht;
flehend nah wie das Gesicht von Hunden,
aber immer wieder weggedreht,

wenn du meinst, sie endlich zu erfassen.
So Entzognes ist am meisten dein.
Wir sind frei. Wir wurden dort entlassen,
wo wir meinten, erst begrüßt zu sein.

Bang verlangen wir nach einem Halte,
wir zu Jungen manchmal für das Alte
und zu alt für das, was niemals war.

Wir, gerecht nur, wo wir dennoch preisen,
weil wir, ach, der Ast sind und das Eisen
und das Süße reifender Gefahr.

Index

First Lines, English

Ah, loose in the wind,	103
Ah, take away from us strikers of hours and counters.	104
And night, and distant movement; for in squads	47
And they say nothing, because the partitions	113
And you wait, you wait for the one	27
A phantom, still, is only like a spot	74
As he prepared to enter her in his need,	81
As if he heard. Silence: a thing far away…	69
As, in the hand, a sulphur match, pale, sends	48
As one spices up a slumbrous drink	85
Avoided by the early-autumn dawn,	82
Bewitched one: how can two selected words	58
Brother Body is poor…: that means, be rich for him.	100
Darkness was like riches in the room	26
Death is great.	91
Distance between stars, how far; and yet how many times farther,	132
For some time I have seen	112
From so much watching of the bars, at last	46
He knew of death only what everyone knows:	90
How all things are afar	22
How have I felt it, what departure means.	65
How it stands there before the darkening	104
How shall I keep my soul here, motionless,	60
I am alive just as the century goes.	15
I am No one and No one I shall be.	28
I am, you anxious man. Do you not hear	4
I come upon you in all of these things	3
I live out my life in widening rings	2
In the deep nights I dig for you, dear treasure.	12

In withered woods there sounds out a bird call,	33
I shall again remember *you*, whom I knew	128
It all rested on her and was the world	54
It was not in me. It went out and in.	25
I wish I could lullaby someone,	32
I would like to develop into one	38
Just as at times from the Master the pressing	129
Just as the king, out hunting, takes a glass,	56
Leaves fall, they fall as from a distant place,	18
Let the world recklessly change	125
Lifting my glance from the book, from the close-up, countable lines,	96
Lightly, as if she has died	76
Like a person lying down, he stands,	68
Like one who has roamed into alien seas,	35
Loneliness is like a rain.	37
Lord: it is time. Summer was fine indeed.	20
Much like, in crucibles, a final green,	57
My life is not this steeply rearing hour	11
My room and this vast thing,	30
Nights are in no sense fashioned for all.	42
Night, silent night, in which are interwoven	41
Oh, how my body blossoms from each vein	116
Oh Lord, give us each his distinctive death.	9
One is, who those alive in his hand takes,	5
Only the one who has raised	121
Path in the garden, deep as a generous draught,	105
Perhaps in heavy mountains I walk here	10
Praise, that's the thing! One well marked out for praise,	120
Put out both eyes of mine: I still can see you,	8
Red barberries assume now their ripe tone,	14
Rides forth the knight in dark-black steel	110
Rose, o sovereign, to people in old days	131
Seldom does a shower of damp mold	86
Shall we reject our ancient friendship, the great	127
She always is thinking: I am…I am…	114

She sat at tea like others, guests and host.	52
Sir, do you hear the New's	124
Springtime has come again. The earth	126
Steadfastness of a longtime noble line	51
Suddenly from all greens of the park	61
Suddenly she steps forth, wrapped in air	84
Summer hums. The late day makes one tired;	80
Summon me to that one of your hours	133
Tears, tears that burst out of me.	95
That is yearning: to dwell in the surges	107
That which the flying birds cast themselves through	94
The bird calls are beginning to sound thanks.	101
The blind man who is standing on the bridge,	36
The evening changes slowly now its garments,	19
The king's hair had been cut;	106
There a tree rose. Oh pure change and abiding!	118
There stands death as a bluish extract in	98
The woods are fragrant again.	40
They every one have weary mouths	24
They had grown used to him, but when the flame	78
This is the animal that does not be.	130
This toil, going through the not-yet-done	50
This work was ordered by the artists' guild.	67
Under a roof and in its shade revolves	70
Violin, stranger, are you following me?	34
Wait…that tastes good…but now it's in flight.	123
We did not know his head, denied us here,	77
We know nothing of this departing, that	62
We waken now amid our memories	97
What, though, restrains us from believing that	64
What will you do, God, when I die?	6
Whoever you are: When evening comes, step out	21
With blossom, vine-leaf, fruit we go our way.	122
Workmen we are: novices, masters, doers,	92
You come and go. The doors slip-to	108
You move away from me, oh Hour.	66

First Lines, German

Ach entzögen wir uns Zählern und Stundenschlägern. 102
Ach, im Wind gelöst, ...103
Als ihn der Gott in seiner Not betrat, ...81
Als ob er horchte. Stille: eine Ferne… 69
Auf einmal ist aus allem Grün im Park 61
Bruder Körper ist arm…: da heißt es, reich sein für ihn. 100
Das alles stand auf ihr und war die Welt 55
Das Dunkeln war wie Reichtum in dem Raume, ...26
Das ist die Sehnsucht: wohnen im Gewoge 107
Da steht der Tod, ein bläulicher Absud 99
Da stieg ein Baum. O reine Übersteigung! 119
Das war der Auftrag an die Malergilde. 67
Der Abend wechselt langsam die Gewänder, ...19
Der blinde Mann, der auf der Brücke steht, ...36
Der König war geschoren; 106
Der Sommer summt. Der Nachmittag macht müde; 80
Der Tod ist groß. 91
Des alten lange adligen Geschlechtes 51
Dich aber will ich nun, *Dich*, die ich kannte...........................128
Die Blätter fallen, fallen wie von weit, ...18
Die Einsamkeit ist wie ein Regen. 37
Die Nächte sind nicht für die Menge gemacht. 43
Diese Mühsal, durch noch Ungetanes 50
Die Vogelrufe fangen an zu rühmen. 101
Du entfernst dich von mir, du Stunde. 66
Du kommst und gehst. Die Türen fallen 109
Durch den sich Vögel werfen, ist nicht der 94
Ein Gespenst ist noch wie eine Stelle, ...75
Er wußte nur vom Tod, was alle wissen: 90
Es war nicht in mir. Es ging aus und ein. 25
Fremde Geige, gehst du mir nach? 34
Frühling ist wiedergekommen. Die Erde 126
Gemieden von dem Frühherbstmorgen, der 83
Hebend die Blicke vom Buch, von den nahen zählbaren Zeilen, 96

Herr: es ist Zeit. Der Sommer war sehr groß.	20
Hörst du das Neue, Herr,	124
Ich bin, du Ängstlicher. Hörst du mich nicht	4
Ich bin Niemand und werde auch Niemand sein.	29
Ich finde dich in allen diesen Dingen	3
Ich lebe grad, da das Jahrhundert geht.	15
Ich lebe mein Leben in wachsenden Ringen	2
Ich möchte einer werden so wie die,	39
Ich möchte jemanden einsingen,	32
Ich sehe seit einer Zeit,	112
Im welken Walde ist ein Vogelruf,	33
In tiefen Nächten grab ich dich, du Schatz.	13
Ist einer, der nimmt alle in die Hand,	5
Jetzt reifen schon die roten Berberitzen,	14
Leicht, wie nach ihrem Tode	76
Lösch mir die Augen aus: ich kann dich sehn,	8
Meine Stube und diese Weite,	31
Mein Leben ist nicht diese steile Stunde	11
Mit einem Dach und seinem Schatten dreht	71
Nacht, stille Nacht, in die verwoben sind	41
Nun wachen wir mit den Erinnerungen	97
Nur wer die Leier schon hob	121
O dieses ist das Tier, das es nicht giebt.	130
O Herr, gib jedem seinen eignen Tod.	9
O wie blüht mein Leib aus jeder Ader	116
O wie ist alles fern	23
Plötzlich tritt sie, in den Wind gehüllt,	84
Reitet der Ritter in schwarzem Stahl	111
Rose, du thronende, denen im Altertume	131
Rufe mich zu jener deiner Stunden,	133
Rühmen, das ists! Ein zum Rühmen Bestellter,	120
Sein Blick ist vom Vorübergehn der Stöbe	46
Selten reicht ein Schauer Feuchter Fäule	87
Sie haben alle müde Münde	24
Sie hatten sich an ihn gewöhnt. Doch als	79
Sie muß immer sinnen: Ich bin… ich bin…	115

Sie saß so wie die anderen beim Tee.	53
Sollen wir unsere uralte Freundschaft, die großen	127
So wie das letzte Grün in Farbentiegeln	57
So wie dem Meister manchmal das eilig	129
So wie der König auf der Jagd ein Glas	56
Tränen, Tränen die aus mir brechen.	95
Und du wartest, erwartest das Eine,	27
Und Nacht und fernes Fahren; denn der Train	47
Und sie schweigen, weil die Scheidewände	113
Verzauberte: wie kann der Einklang zweier	59
Vielleicht, daß ich durch schwere Berge gehe	10
Wandelt sich rasch auch die Welt	125
Wartet…, das schmeckt… Schon ists auf der Flucht.	123
Was aber hindert uns zu glauben, daß	64
Was wirst du tun, Gott, wenn ich sterbe?	7
Weg in den Garten, tief wie ein langes Getränke,	105
Wer du auch seist: Am Abend tritt hinaus	21
Werkleute sind wir: Knappen, Jünger, Meister,	93
Wieder duftet der Wald.	40
Wie einer, der auf fremden Meeren fuhr,	35
Wie ein Liegender so steht er; ganz	68
Wie hab ich das gefühlt was Abschied heißt	65
Wie in der Hand ein Schwefelzündholz, weiß,	49
Wie in einem Schlaftrunk Spezerein	85
Wie soll ich meine Seele halten, daß	60
Wie steht er da vor den Verdunkelungen	104
Wir gehen um mit Blume, Weinblatt, Frucht.	122
Wir kannten nicht sein unerhörtes Haupt,	77
Wir wissen nichts von diesem Hingehn, das	63
Zwischen den Sternen, wie weit; und doch, um wievieles noch weiter,	132

Acknowledgments

I am grateful to these magazines and to an anthology for publishing the following translations from Rainer Maria Rilke:

Untitled ["I live out my life"], *Measure*

The Panther and The Last Evening, *Metamorphoses*

End of Autumn, *The Penn Review*

The Loved One's Death, *Radix*

Autumn, *The Christian Century*

The Swan, Leda, *National Review*

Buddha, *Rhino*

To Music, *The Queens Review*

Untitled ["I am alive"], Untitled ["My life is not"], *Arkansas International*

Woman Going Blind, Sonnets to Orpheus II, 4, *Blue Unicorn*

The Girl Grown Up (Winner of Der Hovanessian Prize for poetry in translation), New England Poetry Club anthology

Corpse-Washing, *Time of Singing*

The Angels, Untitled ["You come and go"], *Off the Coast*

Entrance, *Pensive*

Knight, Archaic Torso of Apollo, *Better Than Starbucks*

A Recollection (published as Remembrance), The Gazelle, People at Night, The Boy, Bridge by the Carousel, *The Bombay Literary Magazine*

At the Brink of Night, *CutBank*

The Neighbor, *Parcham*

Save 20%

on Donald Mace Williams' translation
Beowulf: For Fireside and Schoolroom
using the QR code below.

Look for collections of Donald Mace Williams'
poetry and his memoir, *Being Ninety*,
at StoneyCreekPublishing.com.